D1825168

Vegetable
Growing

Vegetable Growing

FRED W. LOADS

JOHN GIFFORD LTD
LONDON

ISBN 0 7071 0014 3

John Gifford Ltd
125 Charing Cross Road
London, W.C.2H 0EB

First published 1959

© *W. & G. Foyle Limited 1959*

This edition published by John Gifford Ltd 1973

Text set in Times Roman and
printed in Great Britain by the Hope Burgess Group
on Tudor Coated Cartridge. Bound by
James Burn Bookbinders Ltd, Esher

Contents

Red cabbage var. Niggerhead

1 Growing your own vegtables

There must be few people who never eat vegetables but the strange thing is that although the range is so wide many gardeners restrict themselves to the rather more usual varieties.

Some vegetables are eaten raw just as brought in from the garden, others can be cooked in various ways. It is not only the roots of vegetables that are eaten, for in some cases the stem, leaves and even seeds are edible. A rule to observe in vegetable gardens is to grow   7 which you eat and in sufficient quantity to supply anticipated needs. Sow little and often should be the aim. In this way gluts and shortages can often be avoided.

The potato is one of the most important, having come to this country from S. America at the beginning of the Sixteenth Century. For the amateur gardener it is the early varieties that are most worth growing. Also from S. America has come sweet corn or maize which is now highly valued as corn on the cob.

The tomato, too, is usually classed as a vegetable and it came to Britain from South America in the middle of the Sixteenth Century being referred to at that time as the Love Apple. Members of the wide onion family are natives of Egypt and India, whilst beans of various kinds originated in China and S. America.

No vegetable grower would think of doing without onions or carrots. The huge brassica or cabbage family is very wide in the type of vegetable provided, and it is not difficult to make a selection of varieties to last through the year.

It is strange that gardens attached to the modern semi-detached and council houses are often given over entirely to growing decorative plants whereas with a little planning good flavoured health promoting food could be grown.

Vegetables will grow in any soil and in almost any habitable part of the British Isles but, naturally, the better the conditions offered them the better the crops will be. All but the poorest of soils naturally contain all the elements necessary for plant growth and it can be safely assumed that any land which will grow weeds will also grow vegetables.

The greatest enemy of all vegetable plants is a waterlogged soil and this is the reason why all garden writers stress the fact that "soil must be well-drained". Unfortunately, this conjures up visions of deep trenches and masses of pipes, whereas it simply means that the rain water which falls on the soil should be able to get away easily and not stand on the surface.

Water can, of course, come up through the ground and it is when this happens that pipe or field drains are necessary.

In the case of new houses a wet, soggy garden is often due to clay being dug out from a lower level for foundations and for sewers, spread on the surface and covered with good soil, or in reverse piled on the surface over good soil. When this happens, no matter what the site is to be used for, the only real solution is, put the clay back underneath again where it belongs and bring the good dark-coloured soil to the surface.

An alternative is, break up the mass of clay into chunky hunks in the autumn and leave these to break down by the action of weather. A comforting thought for those taking over a new house in spring, is that hot, dry weather will break up clay as effectively as frost.

A garden in which vegetables have been grown previously presents no problem but with a new garden the selection of the vegetable patch is important. Contrary to a widely-held belief, a vegetable garden does not want to be unduly sheltered and screened except in exposed northern districts. Sheltered gardens also shelter pests and in particular, those that fly.

Field crops rarely suffer from pests to the same extent as garden, partly because the adults are more exposed to their natural enemies and because they are not able to alight to lay their eggs when a stiff breeze is blowing.

No matter what type of garden is aquired it is impossible to go wrong with regard to manuring or the application of organic matter, which can be very roughly described as something which once lived. Quite a substantial amount of this can be provided from the garden itself in the form of discarded vegetation such as lawn mowings, old stalks from the herbaceous border, tomato and chrysanthemum stalks from the greenhouse and even clippings from the hedge.

The shortage of farmyard manure need no longer deter anyone from growing tip-top vegetables because there are now organic materials such as 6X 100% which is even better than farmyard manure, especially on slug-infested land.

Much has been written about the value of compost and how to make it, so much that one gets the feeling that making compost is a major operation and a smelly, messy job. Nothing could be farther from the truth. In fact, compost is quite clean and pleasant to handle, encourages the production of good flavoured, disease free crops. The site need not be unsightly as it can be screened in a number of ways, either by a rustic or trellis screen over which climbing roses, jasmine, polygonum, runner beans or loganberries may be trained. No one need be bothered about using fruit trees or bushes as a screen as there is nothing noxious or unpleasant about a compost heap. If there is any smell at all the fault is with the maker. In fact, a bed of cauliflowers or sprouts can smell stronger.

Nothing elaborate is needed, just a space 4ft. × 4ft. with a similar space the same size onto which to turn it. Merely put down a layer of vegetation, leaves, weeds, etc., to a depth of about six inches and cover with a thin layer of soil repeating the process until the heap is 3ft.–4ft. high. When it reaches a sufficient height turn it over and

Vegetable Garden

start another one, the first lot will be ready for use in about six months. The failure to make decent compost is usually due to the failure to make a square-topped heap, a conical heap is useless. A countryman understands the importance of "keeping the corners up" when loading a waggon or making a stack. This is vitally important as once a cone-shaped heap is made it is impossible to put any more on the steep sides. The volume of the heap naturally decreases when a cone is made, the weight is reduced and there is not sufficient material in the pile to cause heating and so the breaking-down process is either slow or never starts.

To overcome this, four posts can be driven into the ground and enclosed by coarse wire mesh, but this is not really necessary if it is remembered to tread the corners and keep them always higher than the centre when building the heap.

In districts of high rainfall it may be necessary to erect a shelter over the top, but in practice this is rarely necessary. As a general rule the debris and waste material from an ordinary garden will not provide sufficient material for digging into the ground and should be supplemented by other available material such as straw, peat etc.

Swiss chard—rhubarb

Supplies will vary according to the district, such as straw in agricultural districts, wool shoddy in Yorkshire, cotton shoddy or devillings in Lancashire, cocoa and tobacco residue. Pond and river weed and sewage is available in nearly every district as well as, of course, an annual supply of dead leaves.

With the exception of peat it is not advisable to dig these materials straight into the ground as such materials which take a long time to decay in the ground actually reduce the amount of nitrogen available to the crops.

Neither is it wise to dig in or throw on the surface such concentrated manures as poultry droppings. Like sewage, this is best composted and mixed with a greater volume of bulkier material like straw. A compost heap should be regarded as the teeth of the garden which chews up the food before it passes to the stomach of the soil. Not the happiest analogy perhaps, but it does serve to illustrate what is meant.

The time taken for the breaking down is very variable and depends on material and time of year; the process being quicker from April to October.

If an abundance of leaves is available they should be used with care as it is rather a pity that the greater the humus content of the soil, the greater the slug population, and masses of dead leaves are the worst of all. They are, however, very valuable not only for potting and making special composts, but for all garden crops and the best way to treat them is work them into the compost heap or treat them separately. Where a large volume is available they can be made to serve two purposes—as a source of heat and as organic material. Mark off an area and stack the damp leaves in a square or rectangular stack and tread firmly as the stack is being built. Dust on to every barrowful of leaves a 4-inch potful of superphosphate; this not only assists in decomposition but kills slugs and adds a vital food to the soil. When the stack is about four feet high, leave for a week or ten days and then turn and restack.

It should then heat up rapidly. Allow to settle for a day or two and then place a portable frame on this and put in about six inches of soil. In this, or in boxes placed on this, seedlings can be grown and salads and carrots can be sown in the soil.

Rhubarb, asparagus and chicory can be forced on such a hot bed and early dwarf beans, cucumbers and melons can be grown to perfection in an apparently primitive medium.

Never overlook this source of heat if there is the slightest chance
of making up a hotbed, as the warm, moist heat generated by fer-

menting materials is much more to the liking of plants than any yet devised by man.

Before the introduction of greenhouses and heating systems, gardeners had to rely entirely on screens of hurdles and straw, oiled silk and canvas and the heat from fermenting manure to produce all their out-of-season fruits and vegetables.

It is, I suppose, human nature for an enthusiastic devotee of a cult to try to convert an unbeliever to see the light and the keen gardener is no exception. Therefore, it must be accepted that the majority of people are only lukewarm gardeners, some maintaining their gardens because they must, for shame's sake. Others may be keen but have only very limited time and means, whilst others like a nice garden if only someone else would do the work.

Much of the monotonous routine can be cut out of gardening by careful thought and by the application of the very rules and principles which they study in their daily work. For instance, a careful, meticulous clerk or engineer in the top flight of his job is often a careless and time-wasting gardener. If only he brought to bear system and time and motion study to his garden, it would leave a great deal more time to enjoy the jobs he liked best and to use the garden as a place in which to really relax and unwind. No-one knows better than the writer how difficult it is to approach a gardening job soberly and leisurely after a day of high pressure activity, with telephones, dictaphones and all the mad rush of modern business life. One of the biggest failings is trying to cultivate too much garden so that it becomes a chore and a millstone. Detailed design is outside the scope of a book on vegetables, but even here the work can be considerably reduced by having a few things ready at once and not a glut and a famine.

No-one can eat two rows of cabbages or lettuces if ready all at once, often four lettuces a week or one cabbage a week is all that is required and yet row upon row is grown by reason of fear that if a few are grown they may be destroyed by pest or disease. Even this fear is taken care of if there is a succession to follow on and if the few pages on the cultivation of lettuce are mastered, the secret will be yours.

Start using vegetables before they are mature and not only enjoy the luxury of crisp young, well-flavoured vegetables but also prevent a glut and a surfeit. So use the wide drill system and intercropping methods advised, treble your returns and halve your labour.

All seeds need to be sown into soil which has been well broken up **Sowing**

Picking peas

and this means well broken up with a fork and not just by raking the surface level. At the same time after the seeds have been sown they need the soil pressing gently but firmly around them, a job which is best done by tamping them down with the head of a rake.

Seeds can be sown even in dust-dry soil without harm if the drills are watered before sowing. On no account should seed be sown first and the ground watered afterwards as this will not penetrate deeply enough and the soil will cake and quickly dry out.

When sowing during dry weather take out a wider and deeper drill than usual and put water gently on the sides washing in a little fine soil. The soil will quickly soak the water up and the seeds can then be sown on this and dry soil pulled over the seed. Do not be tempted to water over the dry surface soil, otherwise the trapped moisture will be quickly drawn to the surface.

Label and mark rows with the date of sowing and variety so that they can be used again, not merely by impaling the packet on a stick: this is very untidy and the packets soon disappear: small metal labels are cheap and easy to use.

Picking sprouts

Weeds   Keeping down weeds in any garden takes more time than the sowing and cultivation of crops, but the control of weeds in a vegetable garden is much easier than anywhere else.

True, certain weeds are blown in from outside sources such as neglected gardens and from waste land. The worst of these is groundsel and although the seeds of dandelions and willow herb drift about all over the place they are not a serious menace to the gardener. Dock seedlings are a nuisance for several years when a new garden has been made on land which was formerly waste ground, and chickweed is a scourge on well-cultivated land rich in nitrogen. Fortunately all these can be reduced very easily by cultivating them. This may be a new approach to many, but a little thought will reveal the advantages of this method.

Through many years of persecution by gardeners, weeds have developed a technique of self-preservation and toughness and an ability to survive and reproduce and seed even when in a dying condition. For instance, hand weeding or the slightest movement of chickweed will cause the seeds to scatter in all directions and in a few days the soil will be green again with seedlings. Groundsel can be hoed up when the flowers are in the bud stage but, even without roots, they have the capacity of flowering and setting and ripening seeds when dying.

To set about cultivating them, in spring, break down and rake fairly finely, soil previously dug in autumn, but do not sow crop seeds. First allow the weed seeds to germinate, then spray or water them with a fine-rosed can, with a solution of Chilean nitrate of soda at the rate of 2–3 ozs. per gallon of water. If done during a bright day the weed seedlings will be completely destroyed in a few hours and the soil will not be harmed in any way as it would if a weed killer or a hormone weed killer were used. This is perfectly harmless and at least half the weed seed population in the upper layer of soil will be destroyed and the crop will get away to a clean start free from weed competition.

Crop seeds may be sown straight away, as it is not necessary to saturate the soil, the object being merely to burn off the foliage of the weed seedlings which in that young state will cause almost instant death. This practice may be continued between the rows during the growing season by using a hooded spray nozzle. A temporary hood can be made from cardboard shaped like a cone, but the handyman can soon make one out of plastic, roofing felt or aluminium.

Beetroot is unaffected by nitrate of soda, so the whole of this crop may be sprayed, thus killing the weeds and stimulating the plants.

16

Celery, carrots, parsnips and parsley can be sprayed in the young stage with a low grade paraffin oil or with a special oil obtainable from seedsmen which will kill seeds and leave the plants unharmed.

Many gardens are infested with a fern-like weed variously known as marestail or horse tail: in fact, Equisetum. This has a very deep root system often going down many feet and is extremely interesting as it is one of the survivors of primeval plants. Many millions of years ago this plant attained a height of some forty feet and was about 4 or 5 ins. in diameter. Basing its age and reduction of size it should disappear about 20 million years hence, but in the meantime it is not really so bad as it is painted, as with its very deep root system it draws up plant food from depths of three and four feet which would otherwise be unavailable to the gardener. It also contains a great deal of silica and if the gardener would cut it off with the hoe or pull it up and leave it on the ground it makes a valuable addition to the food supply in the soil.

Being of a grass-like nature it is not easy to destroy by spraying, but if a solution of hormone weed-killer containing 2-45.T is made up and placed in a shallow basin and the fern-like growth is placed in this, the foliage will absorb it and work down to the roots.

Many pests and diseases breed in hedge bottoms on the wild counterparts of vegetables, so the hedges should be kept trimmed and the banks free from weeds.

Convolvulus in some districts is a nuisance, not only killing hedges but by spreading into the garden. This can be eliminated by spraying in May and June with a hormone weedkiller containing 2-45.T. A concentration of one part in 200 is sufficient, but hedge plants such as hawthorn will stand up to a solution of one part in fifty.

Use always according to instructions and avoid the drift of spray on to neighbouring crops.

The planting of rhubarb or Russian comfrey along the bottom of a hedge will also help to prevent hedge weeds or weeds from waste land adjoining gardens from encroaching. Both these subjects and especially comfrey make wonderful summer hedge and excellent windbreaks and do not harbour pests or diseases.

Swede—Kelvedon Advance

2 Manures and manuring

Much has been written for and against the use of non-organic fertilisers on the soil. In some cases claims have been made that the flavour of fruits and vegetables has been adversely affected, their vitamin content lowered, and that actual harm will befall those who eat them.

There is, fortunately, no real evidence of this. In fact, it is quite possible to grow excellent crops of all kinds without the plants ever touching or seeing soil. Even ordinary garden soil is more complex than the most involved chemical or substance made by man. Not only is it a complete laboratory containing enormous quantities of chemicals, it is teeming with life as well, from wild animals as big as worms to microscopic organisms. In spite of its complexity, experience over centuries has shown there is nothing in it that need worry the ordinary man, it only requiring common sense to get the best out of it. Few of the past generations of mothers knew anything of the mysteries of vitamins and proteins, but by using common sense and by not being carried away by extreme ideas they managed to feed and bring up their families in a healthy, sensible manner.

It is obvious that no person can continue or even start to take and continue to take money out of a bank or a hole in the ground without first putting some there. So it is the same with the soil in the garden. Chemists and analysts have found out over many years of careful research the various chemicals which are found in plants, so it is only logical that it is necessary to put back these same ingredients, or ingredients which will break down and produce these chemicals.

It has been found that animals and birds are an essential link in the process of breaking down organic substances such as corn, grass and various edible seeds. They eat these substances and extract what their bodies need. The residue, plus various additions, passes from

Giant Pumpkin

them as waste and conveniently this is a condition ideally suitable for providing the salts and minerals essential to plant growth. But before the plants can use this material it must be broken down even smaller by countless numbers of organisms before it reaches a stage when it can be of use to the plant.

What is certain is that many of the chemical salts found in animal manure are essential to plant growth, but for a time it seems to matter very little to the plant whether they come from animal or mineral sources, whether they come in the form of nitrogen from blood or bone or from sulphate of ammonia or potash from fishmeal or from sulphate of potash.

Equally, it is certain that the soil organisms and the soil structure itself must have some form of organic matter and whether this comes in the form of decomposed weeds, bracken, pine needles or rhubarb leaves or from manure is again of little importance.

I would ask the reader to consider the arguments for and against the use of chemicals and as to whether all organic manures should be used, and view the matter as applied to their own garden in a sober commonsense way.

If your body was short of iron and the doctor recommended it as a tonic or medicine it would matter little to your body if it absorbed it in the form of sulphate of iron or a bunch of rusty nails soaked in water. Actually it is not so many years ago that this recipe was used. The real danger is the wasteful and indiscriminate use of concentrated fertilisers to the exclusion of complementary organic materials. This, however, is taken care of nowadays by the high cost of all fertilisers.

If small quantities of manure are available such as the bedding from rabbits, goats or a few hens this is best mixed in with garden refuse as such material is a first-class activator, setting off the chain of decomposition in a way which improves the whole bulk of the compost.

Throughout the book references have been made to a complete fertiliser. This is one which contains the three essentials to plant growth; namely, nitrogen, potash and phosphate in varying, or equal proportions. These fertilisers are compounded most carefully for general use or for particular crops such as 'potato manure', 'tomato manure' and so on. In general it is far better to use these than to play about with straight fertilisers such as sulphate of ammonia etc., unless working to a recommended formula.

Formulas are legion and too much attention should not be attached to them unless soil analysis shows that they should be used. Most analysts will give the recommended additives which should be scrupulously followed to obtain the greatest benefit. Each ingredient used has a part to play in providing the raw material which is added to the soil to be converted by the leaves of the plant into food. Thus, nitrogen whether applied as sulphate of ammonia, nitrate of soda, or dried blood is a stimulant as well as encouraging and producing leafy growth and root action. Too much will produce an unbalanced plant with sappy growth. For example, although a cabbage likes a fair proportion of nitrogen, too much will make a big leafy plant with no heart, or with tomatoes, all leaf and stem and little fruit. Nitrate of soda is a valuable stimulant and should be regarded as such and not relied on as a food.

Potash acts as a corrective to this and assists in the development of floral parts and as the heart of a cabbage contains the flowers, a better proportioned plant is built up.

A very useful manure for many purposes is potash nitrate which is very suitable for every crop, containing 15% nitrogen, 10% potash, and 20% sodium and is a natural manure from Chile. Phosphates are essential to all crops and especially to pod crops such as peas and beans and tomatoes and it also materially advances ripening and is particularly useful for applying to crops like tomatoes which may be reluctant to turn red. It has a similar effect on onions and if applied to the soil around the bulbs in August it will ripen them off nicely and set the skins.

Food v. Stimulant.

There are occasions when it is necessary to apply a stimulant to a person or plant as distinct from a food or body-building substance—the difference between brandy and nourishing soup. Thus with a plant: after a long winter, plants such as lettuces and cabbages which have been barely holding their own may need a quick-acting stimulant to get them moving again, or a spell of cold weather in spring may hold them back and for this purpose a substance such as nitrate of soda would be ideal.

Indeed, for general guidance any fertiliser prefixed by the word Nitrate can be regarded as containing this stimulating nitrogen. Plant foods such as contained in manure or materials which have to decay before releasing the essential salts may be regarded more in the nature of foods rather than stimulants.

Stimulants, to be effective, must be readily soluble and so available to the roots, so it is this very quality that makes them unsuitable for digging into the soil in autumn or winter.

21

It may be thought a good idea for example, to scatter sulphate of ammonia on to the soil when digging so that the nitrogen will be there ready and waiting for the plants and seeds. It does not, however, work out in this way as the substances are so soluble the first heavy rain will wash them down through the soil and literally the fertiliser goes down the drain. So all nitrogenous fertilisers should be kept until the roots of the plant can make use of them straight away.

There was never a truer example of the old saying that "you can take a horse to the water but you can't make him drink" than where applied to putting fertiliser into the ground for plants. Any amount can be put in but it can be completely wasted if the plant is not in a condition to take it up and use it.

So, to sum up, use nitrogenous or stimulating fertilisers when the plant is young and a more complete food in adolescence and middle age with a single fertiliser such as phosphate at the end of its life to help it ripen or produce seed. Stimulants at the end of a plant's life would be wasted and if applied to vegetables at the end of the season during the warmth and moisture of an Indian summer the resultant growth would be so soft that at the first touch of frost the cells would be so charged with sap that they would freeze very quickly, burst and then rot.

The following is a short list of the many fertilisers and materials which are available to gardeners.

Basic Slag.
This is a by-product of the iron and steel industry and contains lime as well as phosphates. It is very slow-acting and should be applied at the time of winter digging and is most beneficial on heavy soils for all garden crops.

Bonemeal (Steamed).
A most valuable long-lasting, slow-acting organic fertiliser, made from bones of animals and birds and steamed to remove the grease and fat which would further slow up decomposition. Dig in winter.

Bonemeal (Raw).
As above, but lasts longer in the soil as the fat in it slows up decay. Ideal to put into beds such as vine borders or asparagus beds which cannot be dug over for many years. Dig in winter.

Bone Flour (Steamed).
A fine dust which can be applied in spring and because of its fineness

is more readily available more quickly. Apply in spring raked into the top two or three inches.

Calcium Cyanamide.
A quick-acting nitrogenous fertiliser containing lime, but because of its dusty nature is not widely used for general application. For the home gardener its most valuable use is in the compost heap, as it breaks down vegetation and materially adds to the value of the heap.

Dried Blood and Blood Products.
These are quick-acting organic stimulants and are best used in this form rather than to pour on fresh blood which is available in some areas. They are leaf and root-producing substances and should only be given to growing plants.

Fish Meal.
A good all-round organic fertiliser containing nitrogen, potash and phosphates and for anyone who objects to the use of chemical fertilisers this can be recommended for all garden uses. As the nitrogen is readily available its use should not be overdone, but full instructions for use are given on the container.

Guano.
This is a natural product and is made by grinding the rock-like deposits of the droppings of sea birds, probably the quickest-acting of all the nitrogenous fertilisers. Apply only to growing plants in spring and summer.

Hoof and Horn Meal.
A slow-acting organic manure which, although slow-acting, contains mostly nitrogen which it gives up over a fairly long period. Rather wasteful for ordinary garden use and is more economically used in seed and potting composts. Mainly autumn and winter.

Kainit.
A rather crude form of potash containing a quantity of impurities and best applied in autumn or winter. Very useful on light soils which are as a rule deficient in potash.

Meat and Bone Meal.
Is a very valuable organic manure containing phosphates and nitrogen, long-lasting and is most beneficial to all garden crops. Apply in autumn and winter.

Muriate of Potash.
Contains a great deal more potash than Kainit but still more crude than sulphate of potash. Good samples contain most potash of all potash fertilisers but needs to be applied to the soil in autumn and winter preferably on the surface. Ideal for onion beds.

Nitrate of Potash.
Better known as saltpetre, rich in potash and nitrogen and should be used in liquid form when the plants are about a third-part grown. Use sparingly and only in solution. Especially useful to the exhibitor to give size and quality.

Nitrate of Soda.
A purely nitrogenous stimulant, quick-acting fertiliser for use on growing plants in solution or a pinch around each plant during showery weather.

Nitro Chalk.
Another quick-acting stimulant and as it contains lime, is most valuable for use on brassicas.

Potash Nitrate.
Mentioned in text.

Soot.
Mainly nitrogenous depending on the source, should not be used in the vicinity of large towns—ideal for country districts as a source of liquid fertiliser especially if used in combination with liquid derived from animal sources. Also acts as a pest deterrent. It is advisable to store for 2–3 months in a dry shed before using. Gives a rich dark colour to foliage.

Sulphate of Potash.
A quick, safe potash fertiliser which can be applied to soil and plants at any time.

Sulphate of Ammonia.
A quick-acting nitrogenous manure for any crop. Apply only to growing crops, dry or in solution, either alone as a stimulant, preferably in combination with sulphate of potash and superphosphate.

24

Superphosphate.
Quick-acting phosphatic manure with a lot of it not soluble in water so holds in the soil a long time. Can be used at any time alone or in combination.

The last three fertilisers contain essentials of all plant growth and most compound fertilisers contain these in varying proportions.

If this fertiliser was regarded as the main plank in any fertilising programme, and small quantities selected from the above list to bolster up, stimulate, or make good any deficiency peculiar to the soil, the gardener would be well on the road to success.

Wood ash and all products of the combustion of organic matter and even the burning of clay are all valuable in the garden and can be applied to the surface at any time of the year and so save storing. Wood ashes or any other burnt materials are particularly valuable when dug into heavy soils as the small pieces of charcoal as well as the ash help to sweeten the soil.

Under modern conditions, unfortunately, little will be available even when trees are pruned as the thicker pieces will be used for fuel. Only twigs from prunings and diseased materials should be burned, garden fires should not be used to get rid of hedge prunings as these are of more value in the compost heap than as ashes.

Mixed vegetables

3 What to grow for kitchen and Exhibition

It is seldom a satisfactory approach to the art of exhibiting even at the smallest of local shows if reliance is placed on the selection of the best vegetable that happens to be available.

Schedules are issued as early in the year as possible to enable exhibitors to lay their plans and to select their varieties. This, I know, savours too much like making a business out of a spot of gardening mainly intended to be a pleasurable hobby.

The art of growing, however, is nothing more than just trying to grow crops well and even the most conscientious gardener would not claim that he had done everything in his power to do the best for his crops all the time. So, to the would-be exhibitor, it is suggested that if it is not possible to make a real fuss of everything then one or two crops should be picked out for special attention. A gardener will soon get to know which crops suit his particular soil best. It may be peas, onions, beans or celery, but there are few gardens where some particular crop does not grow better than another.

It would be doing the reader a disservice to tell him that there are magic potions and devices which will make the produce from any old garden into those magnificent specimens one sees at our great shows, and yet amateurs can and do grow vegetables and flowers as well as any full-time professional.

1st Prize Vegetable, at R.H.S. Show

The first essential is a good strain of a good variety and we have in this country some of the finest seed firms in the world and on whose strains and selections the utmost reliance can be placed.

These then should be sown, grown, planted and cared for as advised, maintaining the soil at the highest peak of fertility by the methods suggested.

Artichokes   You either like Artichokes or you don't and the majority of folk don't because they have never tried them. Apart from any claims as an agreeable vegetable they have other uses in a garden—decorative and utility and surely this can apply to few vegetables.

So if you approach these vegetables warily, set out with the idea of using them as an adornment and useful plant to have in the garden.

The two main types are Globe and Jerusalem, the globe being the one with decorative silvery leaves and a flower head like a big thistle.

I used to think what a waste of time and space it was to grow these big plants to get a few heads off the top, until I found they made most attractive plants in the herbaceous border for screening an unsightly corner or building. With their large leaves and a height of 6 feet or more, the leaves revealing an attractive grey silver underside in the slightest breeze, they make a perfect foil to summer flowers. This is, I think, the best place for them in an ordinary domestic garden.

The Globe   Is a perennial and can be grown from seed sown in the spring, or
Artichoke   small plants may be obtained. Allow 3 feet from the nearest plant or shrub as they get pretty big, but as they are best split up and divided every 3–4 years, treat as an ordinary herbaceous perennial giving the same good treatment with regard to soil preparation.

To cook, cut off the thistle-like heads, trim off the prickly leaf tips, soak for half an hour in tepid salted water, boil till tender, about half an hour for large heads, drain and serve with butter.

They need a little protection in the winter, but if the leaves are put over the crown and tied in position in late autumn this suffices in most districts.

Varieties

White and Purple Globe, the purple being more suitable for northern
28   gardens.

These crop at the bottom like potatoes which they resemble in several ways. The tops are, however, much like sunflowers and if a row is planted on the windward side of a garden make an excellent windbreak.

They do need a well-drained soil and treatment as would be given to potatoes in the matter of manuring, otherwise the tubers come so small that they are not worth cooking.

The recipe book should be studied before cooking, for although they make an excellent soup and can be used in several ways, if they are just plain boiled you will be put off them for ever.

My favourite way is the same as for parsnips, cut into large chips, partly boil, dry and fry golden brown in deep fat.

Lift as required, save a few tubers for seed, dig in compost and re-set about 1ft. apart. Try to get up all the small ones or the row will be choked with small useless growths. They require no staking or attention during the growing season except a dose of fertiliser and as previously stated have a claim in a windy garden as an effective windbreak.

Jerusalem Artichokes

Easy to grow on well cultivated light soil this crop likes the sun. The spirally twisted tubers vary in length from 1 to 3 in. and at their widest part are about an inch thick. They mature from November onwards and should be dug as required. Use as soon as lifted and do not allow them to remain in the light or they will become discoloured.

Chinese Artichokes

The last thirty-five years has seen a great levelling out of social distinctions and many things which were the prerogative of one class are now shared more widely.

Curiously enough, the type of what might be called luxury vegetables has increased very little. Asparagus could be placed in this category and fewer asparagus beds are laid down now, partly because of the space the beds or rows occupy in relation to the size of the ordinary garden and partly because of the length of time that must elapse from seed to cutting. This is another crop which can be grown in the flower garden if the temptation to cut the decorative foliage in summer can be resisted.

Asparagus may be grown as a single row crop and in this way does not occupy so much space as would a bed. The raised bed certainly has advantages especially in wet districts or where the soil is thin.

Asparagus

29

Beds are best prepared some months in advance of planting which should be done in April. First mark out one bed about 4ft. wide and as long as is convenient. Double dig this and add as much manure as possible, then dig out a path-like strip on either side about 2ft. wide and spread this soil on the bed. Into this work bonemeal and muriate of potash at 3ozs. and 2ozs. per sq. yd. respectively. Do this some months in advance of planting and allow to settle. Work in old mortar rubble or crushed limestone, using an ordinary bucketful for 6 sq. yds. On light soils use half this quantity. Salt is beneficial, particularly on light sandy soils, a dressing of an ounce to the square yard in mid April being followed after a three week interval by another smaller amount.

As it takes three years from seed before the plants are big enough to plant out, it pays to buy in three-year-old plants, even then no cutting must be taken the season following planting.

Subsequent cultivation consists of keeping the bed free from weeds and keeping the soil fertile either by giving a spring dressing of manure or by watering during the growing season, with liquid manure.

Row cropping is no different from planting out a row of lettuces, allow a space of 2ft. 6ins. on each side of the row and space the plants at about 15ins. apart—spacing in the bed the same, i.e., 15ins. from plant to plant. Never cut after the end of June, but allow the foliage to develop, cutting this down in November.

Clumps of fine plants dotted about in the herbaceous border will provide several boilings of the exquisitely flavoured vegetable and later in the year the fern-like foliage looks really attractive amongst the summer flowers. If this foliage is snipped for use in vases in the house, grow a few plants separately for this purpose, as the result of foliage cutting is to make the edible heads smaller each year.

Connovers Colossal is the most widely grown variety but other good sorts are Argenteuil, Kidners strain and White Cap.

Aubergine (Egg plant) Is a popular vegetable with those who have sampled it abroad and who have taken the trouble to grow it for the first time.

In the southern half of the country it may be grown outdoors or under cloches and will thrive on a warm, sheltered border under conditions suitable for tomatoes. The seeds should be sown in gentle in spring and potted up separately in 3-inch pots and if to be grown in a porch or greenhouse pot up when the pot is full of roots into a 7-inch or 8-inch pot.

30

Plant outdoors under cloches in late April or early May—after frosts have gone, if unprotected after first hardening on

Each plant will produce an average of eight egg-shaped fruits, purple in colour. This variety is ripe when the fruit is uniformly coloured. This fruit is rarely used as a vegetable by itself, but by cutting lengthwise and scooping out the centre like a small marrow and stuffing with any meat or poultry filling available.

Syringe to keep free from greenfly, and occasionally when in flower, to set the fruit. Using a fine spray from a hose is quite sufficient for this purpose.

Beans

There is enough variety in these to provide a different one every day for a fortnight, but this treat is only available for those who grow their own, as only poor samples of three of the better known varieties are ever available in shops.

The treatment for all varieties of bean is fundamentally the same; a well drained soil, not too much animal manure, but plenty of phosphates which can be supplied in the form of bonemeal or superphosphate are their main requirements. Some of the more tender types may be limited to the southern counties, unless cloche protection is given in the early stages, due more to the shortness of the northern growing season than for any other reason.

Elaborate and deeply dug trenches are sometimes made for beans, but if the soil is in a decent condition this is unnecessary. In fact on heavy clay soils unless a trench is well made and drained it may become a grave for the plants.

Beans being legumes have the capacity of producing nitrogen-fixing nodules on their roots and actually add to the manurial value of soil, a fact which is used advantageously by the practice of cutting off tops after the crop has finished and following it with a leaf producing crop which enjoys the extra nitrates.

Broad Beans

These are the hardiest of the beans, but do not enjoy the popularity they deserve because the pods are often allowed to stay too long on the plants, whilst beans bought on the market can give the beginner little idea of flavour of young beans boiled in the liquor in which bacon or a ham shank has been cooked.

In the southern half of England seeds may be sown in autumn and the resultant plants allowed to stand outdoors all winter to produce an early crop.

This practice is designed not only for earliness in cropping, but so that they will reach a stage where black fly, the worst enemy of the broad bean, can do them no harm.

It is often recommended that seeds of broad beans be sown at six inches apart in a double row, but as they make an excellent wind-break and are one of the first vegetable crops to be sown, four rows instead of two provide more beans at a time when they are most welcome and give protection to any other early crops. The actual sowing date will vary with the district and soil, but it can be generally be reckoned that for all practical purposes the first sowings can be made in the south in February and about a month later in the northern half of the country.

There are two types and many varieties, the types are Longpod and Windsor. The Longpod being the hardiest is the type which should be sown in autumn for overwintering. The Windsors are better flavoured.

Good varieties include: Longpods—Longfellow, Exhibition Longpod and Gillett's Imperial Longpod. Red Epicure is a distinct Longpod type, the rich chestnut-crimson seeds making it distinct, although these change to straw-colour when cooked. Windsors—Imperial Windsor, White and Green Windsor.

The easiest way to sow the seed is to make a shallow trench 2 inches deep, scatter some bonemeal or superphosphate on the bottom of trench and work it into the top inch or so with a fork. Tamp the surface of the disturbed soil with the head of a rake held vertically and sow on the levelled soil.

Mice and slugs sometimes attack the beans when they become softened after a few days in the soil. These may be deterred by dusting soot or peat soaked with Jeyes' scattered over the surface immediately after sowing.

Subsequent cultivation consists of keeping them free from weeds, and in windy districts it may be necessary to put in a few stakes and stretch string along each side of the row. A close watch must be kept for black aphis which appears on the tender new growths and it is for this reason that it is advised to pinch out the top or growing point. This top, by the way, is an excellent vegetable and can be boiled and eaten like cabbage or other green vegetable.

A certain care in timing is necessary for this, for if pinched out too early or too low down some of the blossom buds may be removed as well. On the other hand if delayed too long the fly may get established and be difficult to get rid of. A spray containing B.H.C. or Pyrethrum insecticide is probably the best to use as these have a deterrent effect.

These are a prolific crop and have the advantage that any surplus beans can be preserved for winter use either frozen, salted or bottled. They can be used as an ornamental screen over a trellis or up a wall or grown as clumps in a flower border like sweet peas. Not nearly enough use is made of this flower-cum-vegetable arrangement, as in the case of runner beans some varieties have brick red flowers, one called Painted Lady is a bi-colour white and red, and Blue Lake an excellent stringless variety has bright blue flowers

For ordinary use any well-drained soil will suit them, but for exhibition purposes extra manure should be dug into a strip about 2ft. wide. When planted near a wall care must be taken to see that they do not dry out at the roots or they will not set the beans. Flower dropping often occurs during a period of dry weather, but a syringing or a spray over the foliage in the evening will help to cure this tendency.

Runners are not so hardy as broad beans and consequently cannot be sown until danger of frost is past and in the north this is a great disadvantage. Fortunately, it is easy to overcome this by sowing seeds thickly in a box of equal parts soil, peat and sand, placing them in a greenhouse, cold frame or even under cloches to germinate and then plant them out in their cropping positions in May.

They may be sown in single or double rows or in clumps, and as they will grow up thin poles, pea sticks or string they are very adaptable. Three sticks or 7ft. canes may be arranged wigwam fashion and the tops tied together or two single rows planted 2ft. apart and the stakes inclined inwards. The advantage is that the beans will hang straight and clear of the supports and will not become blemished, an important matter for the exhibitor.

Where no sticks or only short supports are available—say 2ft. high, allow the plants to climb up these and then cut the tops off. If they are allowed to just be on the ground, the beans are gritty, badly curled and in a wet season will rot.

During the growing season they, like all other crops, respond to a weekly application of liquid manure, but except when grown for exhibition, seldom get this. They must have moisture at the roots, however, hence the advice to add more manure to retain it.

A mulch of manure, compost, peat or grass mowings along each side of the row and close up to the stem will greatly benefit the crop.

Varieties
Prizetaker for exhibition, Kelvedon Wonder, early medium sized pods, Painted Lady—bi-colour for screens and, of course, for

Broad beans

cropping. Streamline and Yardstick are two excellent all-purpose varieties. Blue Lake, stringless oval pods, especially grown for bottling or deep freeze.

Climbing French

This is a variant of the ordinary French or dwarf bean, it is not so vigorous as the scarlet runner but has the merit of producing about three times the number of beans to a given area as does the dwarf variety.

Particularly useful in a cool or unheated greenhouse it crops earlier, more heavily and over a longer period than the dwarf French. Climbing beans can be grown in large pots and boxes or in the soil like tomatoes and enjoy the same soil conditions. I strongly advise growing this bean outdoors in the south and under glass in the north.

There are few varieties, a good one being The King. The large white butter beans can also be grown, but crop very lightly with only two or three beans per pod. French Beans, Haricots and all dwarf beans must be regarded as tender subjects which cannot be relied on to grow satisfactorily outdoors in every part of the country. Where frost-free weather comes late they can be raised in green-

Royalty beans

houses, cold frames or under cloches and should have much the same treatment as dahlias. They will, of course, go ahead then and in a normal season almost as well as in the warmer counties.

Seeds are sown directly into the ground in double rows and spaced about 9 inches apart, a few extra being sown so that the resultant spare plants can be used to fill in gaps caused by losses.

Dwarf Beans Are an excellent and profitable cloche crop as the plants are much larger with longer beans than when grown wholly outdoors, and anyone who has had difficulty in getting a worthwhile crop should give partial or entire protection.

They revel in warmth, provided there is sufficient moisture at the roots, an attribute which makes them ideal subjects for growing for early use in a warm greenhouse.

Six plants can be accommodated in a 10-inch pot sowing the seeds directly into the soil or as previously advised thickly in a box and transplant when the first leaf is formed.

One of the most tender and probably the finest in flavour is the golden wax pod bean and I find this makes an ideal edging to tomatoes when they are grown on a raised bench. Simply press in the seed about 2 inches deep, about 9 inches apart, and when they grow allow them to hang downwards over the edge of the benches In this way they will not interfere with the main crop, in fact the tomatoes will benefit from the association.

It is convenient to grow all the dwarf beans in the same way, i.e. to take out a shallow drill about 2 inches deep and the width of a spade in soil which has been previously well dug and manured. See *Scarlet Runners*.

To exhibitors and those who like to grow something different and appreciate the subtlety of flavour available, I commemd the following types, all of which are obtainable in this country and can be grown easily in the south and with partial or complete protection in the colder districts.

The Shelleasy, dwarf, early, red mottled pods and seed, use green as french bean, dry seed for winter use.

Tiny green snap bean, miniature bean, the whole pods being used.

The best varieties for general use are Masterpiece, The Prince and the selected strain of Canadian Wonder. A new variety named Glamis raised in Scotland is proving particularly suitable for the northern part of the British Isles and is also useful for freezing.

Blue Coco is more or less of a novelty having deep blue pods and flowers. Of excellent flavour the beans can be cooked whole.

36

Beet is a vegetable which is far too often regarded solely as one to store for winter use. This is due partly to force of habit and partly because insufficient are grown for them to be used freely throughout the summer months when they are small, young and tender, and certainly the best flavoured.

This need not be so because the seed is cheap enough, the crop takes up little room and is free from pests.

Although usually boiled and used cold as a salad or a pickle it can be used as a hot vegetable going excellently with fish. As it is a root crop with the edible portion forming under the soil it is essential that the soil in which it is grown should be free from lumps and fresh manure. An impression has arisen that manure need not be added to soil for root crops, but if it is applied early as well-rotted stuff it is quite all right to use it without any fear of the roots becoming forked.

Beetroot bolts easily—that is, runs to seed prematurely without forming a swollen edible root. This is invariably caused by a check to the root system and is nearly always the result of sowing the seed too early in the season. Early May is quite soon enough to sow unprotected, under cloches it may be sown a month earlier. Beetroot seedlings, in fact seedlings of practically all root crops, do not pay for transplanting. They will transplant, but unless it is skilfully done and the weather conditions are suitable, the results will be disappointing. The usual practice is to sow in V-shaped drills and thin out the plants to 6–8 inches apart, but by using this method many seedlings are pulled out and discarded, as a so-called beet seed is not really a seed but a capsule containing two or three shiny black seeds.

A better way is to take out a drill about the width of a spade, much as for beans but only an inch deep, and as an inch is only the width of a halfpenny care must be taken to see that the drill is not made too deep or the seeds will germinate badly. Scatter the seeds thinly along the bottom of the wide drill and cover with fine soil by drawing it over them with the back of a rake.

If the seeds are spaced correctly it will not be necessary to thin the beetroot until they are about the size of golf balls and big enough to eat. By using this method for all the root crops, three and a half times more vegetables can be grown in practically the same space.

When thinning, all that it is necessary to do is to increase the distance between each plant until they all stand at 6–8 inches from plant to plant, and it will be found that after eating young vegetables all the summer there will still be more to store than if a single row had been sown.

Beetroot

The beetroot family are natives of the seashore and benefit from an occasional dressing of salt, about an ounce to the yard of row twice during the growing season, once when about 4 inches high and again when half-grown.

The foliage is so resistant to salty sprays that they can be sprayed overhead with a solution of nitrate of soda 2ozs. to a gallon of water. This should be done when about 2ins. high and will effectively kill out all weeds except those related to the beetroot. Sometimes black fly will attack the foliage and should be sprayed with Derris or B.H.C. insecticide.

When pulling for use, twist off the tops, rinse under a tap and boil. When lifting in the autumn to store, ease up the roots with a fork to avoid breaking the tap root or the severed roots will bleed and the colour and flavour will suffer. Store in sand in boxes or barrels or in a clamp covered with straw in the garden.

The two most suitable types for the garden are Globe and Intermediate, the long-rooted varieties are only suited for light soil and in many households present a problem as they need a very large pan for cooking as they must not be cut before cooking. The exception is Dells Non Bleeding which is a good dark type and can be cut into convenient pieces before putting into the pan.

Sprouts

Globe varieties should be grown for summer and autumn use and intermediate or oval varieties for storing for winter use. Beetroot with their richly coloured tops can be introduced into many a bedding scheme either as dot plants or as a row with contrasting foliage and in this way beauty and utility may be combined, and is a solution when there is neither space nor inclination to have a separate vegetable garden.

Varieties
Detroit Globe, Crimson Globe, Boltardy. A new variety known as Golden beet is now available. Of globe shape, the skin is golden orange and the flesh yellow. It does not 'bleed' like red varieties and can be cooked in the usual way, while the leaves can be boiled and served like spinach.

Brassicas This collective name is being used more every year and is a convenient way of referring to all the many members of the cabbage family as they all require practically the same treatment and are subject to the same pests and diseases, and for all practical purposes respond to the same treatment.

In this large family of cruciferous plants—four petalled or cross-shaped flowers—are also included quite a lot of garden flowers such as stocks and wallflowers as well as weeds such as shepherds purse.

It is particularly important to remember this, as weeds can become host plants on which pests and diseases breed and which migrate to the crop plants. From a cultural angle, avoid planting out seedling wallflowers and stocks in the vegetable garden on land recently occupied by a vegetable crop.

In nearly all cases it is the flower buds of the brassica which are eaten, notably in the case of cauliflowers, sprouts and cabbage whereas in kale the leaves are eaten.

This affects to a certain degree the cultivation, as although it is necessary to make the leaves of the plant grow, if they are encouraged to do so by giving too much nitrogen in the form of substances like sulphate of ammonia, leaves will be made at the expense of firm hearts, and cabbages will be loose, and instead of tight sprout buttons, they will be loose rosettes instead.

Most brassicas need a firm or even a hard soil for the same reason—a loose soil, loose hearts; the exception to this is the cauliflower which needs more fuss made of it than any of the others.

40

Raising Plants.

Seeds of all except cauliflowers are very cheap and as plants are easy to raise from seed it is always best to do this. The advantage of this is that no diseases or pests are imported as often happens when they are brought in, but probably more important is that when home raised, seeds may be sown at intervals so that the crops are spread out over a longer period instead of there being a lot ready at one time, with the inevitable wastage.

Both of these need a very long season of growth and can be sown as early as September of the preceding year and over-wintered in the seed bed and planted out in early April or they can be raised in heat in the greenhouse in January and pricked off into boxes and hardened off in frames. To provide continuity, further sowings may be made in a cold frame and again later outdoors in March, but for the ordinary householder a small sowing in early March and another at the beginning of April will usually suffice. Any sheltered odd corner will provide a seed bed, provided the soil is well-drained and open in texture. No animal manure is necessary for seedlings, but an egg-cupful of superphosphate per sq. yd. dusted on the surface and raked in will promote root formation. This preparation should be done a few days before the actual sowing to allow the soil to settle naturally.

Sprouts and Pickling Cabbages

When larger quantities of seedlings are required special seed beds may be made—see under *Seedbeds.*

Do not leave the plants in the boxes or seed rows too long but get them out into their cropping quarters when from 4 to 6 inches high. On a well dug, well manured soil which has been limed within the last two years, allow 2ft. 6ins. between plants and between the rows. Plant with a dibber and firm each plant well in by treading rather by jabbing with the dibber. During the growing season keep the soil well hoed, not only to prevent weeds developing, but aerate the soil which will stimulate root growth.

Sprouts are a grand crop for cleansing and breaking up new land, the regular hoeing will check the weeds and later when the leaves grow big they will smother out any competition whilst the strong fibrous roots will frustrate and break up the stiffest soil.

In the autumn, remove dead and yellowing lower leaves to allow air to circulate and also cut off any hopelessly blown or burst rosettes. There is no point in allowing useless foliage on the plant to drain away nourishment. Always keep the soil firm around the plant as the wind and rain will rock the heavy-topped plant and loosen its

41

hold in the soil. To offset this tendency, draw up soil around the stems with a hoe in late September.

Even on good soils sprouts will benefit from two or three applications of a complete fertiliser, such as National Growmore, during the growing season. Fit this in the period extending from a month after planting out until the end of September. Later application will result in soft growth which will not stand up to wintry weather.

When gathering sprouts remove the bottom ones first leaving the tops until last when they make excellent spring greens. When the crop has finished do not allow them to flower and seed, but pull up the plants and chop all the soft parts up into small pieces with a sharp spade and dig into the ground and follow on with potatoes. The green material in the soil will keep the potatoes free from scab which disfigures the skin. Discard, of course, the tough woody root and put aside for burning or bury deeply, as they may be affected by club root.

Pests and Diseases.
These are common to all members of the cruciferous family, but the three most serious are a fungus-club root, cabbage root maggot and caterpillars. Fortunately, sprouts and kales are less liable to attack by root maggot than any other member, but these three main troubles will be treated under this heading.

Club Root.
When attacked by this disease the roots become knotted and swollen and eventually decay to a putrid mass and the top becomes stunted and useless.

There are only partial cures for this disease, but a great deal can be done to prevent it getting hold, firstly by keeping the soil in a high state of fertility and by avoiding the growing of successive crops belonging to this family on the same ground.

Control may be effected by dusting the hole at planting time with 4 per cent Calomel dust and by soaking the ground with Jeyes' fluid beforehand and give regular waterings with it during the growing season. This is especially useful as it keeps off the female of the cabbage root fly and if sprayed on the foliage will deter the cabbage white butterfly from laying her eggs. This homely specific is so useful in the garden that it will be mentioned quite a lot as a safe and easily obtainable pest deterrent.

Lime which is a mild fungicide is essential to the growth and well-being of this large family and is especially necessary to keep down club root but as this also helps in the rapid breakdown of any organic matter in the soil, it will be appreciated that the application of lime in greater quantities means constant attention to manuring. Special attention to garden hygiene is very necessary. For example, the burning or burying deeply of affected plants to prevent the spread and distribution of the fungus.

Cabbage Root Maggot.
The maggot or grub is the result of the eggs laid by a small fly near the stem of the plant at intervals during spring and early summer. The eggs hatch out and burrow into the underground portion of the stem, destroying the root system, and ultimately the foliage turns a steely-blue green and the whole plant collapses and dies. Usually by the time this happens the plants are beyond hope and little or nothing can be done about it. In this case, prevention is absolutely essential and there is nothing better for this purpose than peat impregnated with neat Jeyes' fluid at the rate of about a pint to a two-gallon bucket of granulated peat. Scatter this in a six-inch circle around the stems of the seedlings after planting and renew the application at intervals until the end of June when the risk of attack is reduced.

In some areas where this pest is very bad and especially in dry weather, this will be found to be the only way to grow cauliflowers which are particularly susceptible. It will also keep slugs away.

Caterpillars.
These are all too well-known to need description and are the progeny of those white butterflies which flit aimlessly about the garden on sunny days. They lay eggs in clusters on the underside of the leaves, bright orange in colour, which can be easily detected if the leaves are turned up every few days. If these are rubbed over with the finger it will save a lot of grief in a few days' time when they hatch out and eat steadily everything before them. They may be discouraged from laying their eggs by spraying with Derris, B.H.C., or Jeyes' and after the small caterpillars have hatched out too, but the older they get the harder they are to kill as they take evasive action by dropping to the ground.

In recent years much work has been done in the improvement of the strains of brussels sprouts and every seed firm has their own speciality.

For the small or windy garden, dwarf varieties should be chosen especially as this type produces those small to medium, hard little sprouts that can be eaten whole. 43

Varieties.

Fillbasket, Cambridge No. 5. Irish Elegance and Peer Gynt, the latter being an F.1. hybrid.

A novelty is the red brussels sprout. This is quite red in colour and although perhaps not as prolific as the green varieties, has a nutty flavour.

Broccoli   Considerable confusion exists about these and many people regard them as a separate group, whereas in fact, the single-headed types are merely winter heading cauliflowers which have been selected for their hardness and the incurving protective habit of their leaves. The true broccoli are the sprouting types which will be dealt with under its appropiate heading.

To make the fullest use of the successful heading characteristics of the wide range of varieties now offered, a study should be made of several catalogues as it is apt to be confusing as they are divided into three groups: winter heading, early spring heading and late spring heading.

It is further confused by the fact that many of the varieties offered are not hardy in all parts of the country, many being confined in practice to the Scilly Isles, Cornwall and the warmer wintered south. Even where they are hardy in the Northern Counties, proximity to industrial towns will cause heavy losses amongst varieties which will survive in areas just as cold, but in the purer air of the country.

Varieties.

For autumn and winter use: Snow's Winter White, Veitch's Self-protecting, Knight Protecting. For spring use: Leamington, Markanta, For late or summer use: Royal Oak, May Blossom, Midsummer and Late Queen.

Sow from March to June as advised for sprouts and treat culturally in the same way during the growing season.

Broccoli, Sprouting   These produce masses of small heads over a long period and are cut as required. Some varieties produce a large terminal head and after this is cut it is succeeded by a lot of small heads extending over a long season. Their popularity is not so great as they deserve, mainly perhaps because of their rather messy look when over-cooked; their flavour, however, is excellent and supplies are provided over a

44

long period when choice vegetables are scarce. Treatment as for sprouts.

Varieties.
Early and Late white sprouting. Early and Late purple sprouting. Calabrese and Express Corona, green sprouting.

Borecole or Kale

These are the Cinderellas of the brassica family, perhaps because they will grow anywhere and in any soil, and in fact certain types can be found growing wild. They are useful, however, in that they are very hardy indeed and can be relied on to survive very severe winters, producing good quality tender greens when growth starts in spring.

There are several varieties, some with crinkled leaves, plain leaves, others with variegated foliage which looks most attractive in a bed or in the herbaceous border. A few plants of dwarf curly kale is an excellent standby in any garden for household use or for small stock and poultry. For planting in or near large industrial towns with a highly polluted atmosphere, a plain-leaved Kale is best, as the curly ones trap the dirt which is difficult to wash out.

Varieties.
Hungry Gap, Marrow Stemmed, and Thousand Headed are strong, large types and are out of place in all but large gardens, but do provide young tender greens in spring. One further advantage is that they resist the attacks of pests and diseases better than any other member of the family.

Dwarf Green Curled and Asparagus or Buda Kale are two worthwhile varieties, the variety Labrador is the hardiest, whilst Chou de Russie and variegated Kales are useful as well as decorative. Sow in seed beds in March and April and plant out 2ft. apart in June and July; treat generally as sprouts.

Cauliflower

This is the queen of the brassica tribe and needs handling more sympathetically and needs to be fussed over more than any of the others. For instance, sprouts, kales and cabbages can be dropped in a hole made by a dibber and firmed with the heel, but to do it justice the young cauliflower planted should be lifted with a trowel taking with it a ball of soil adhering to the roots.

The cauliflower is the only member of this family which is worthwhile growing under glass in cloche, frame or greenhouse in and out of season.

45

Kale—dwarf curled

Seeds may be sown from January onwards and pricked out in boxes and later transferred to their final quarters and for later outdoor sowings, if sown in drills in April, the young plants are best transferred to nursery beds of good rich soil and spaced about 4 inches apart. Later, when about 6 inches high and have made a good root they may be planted out in very well-manured soil, less firm in texture than for other types.

Being more succulent it is the first attacked by pests and diseases and steps should be taken as advised to ward off attacks. Any check either from drought or pest attacks will almost certainly result in premature buttoning, i.e. the formation of small, ill-flavoured curds, long before they are really ready. So treat the cauliflower like a lady and she will respond. In the cropping plan it will be noticed that the earliest plantings are shielded from cold winds by rows of broad beans and is well worth consideration, particularly in the north.

Varieties are legion, but the beginner or anyone uncertain as to what to grow should try the variety All the Year Round. Sown at intervals one variety can be used for spring and autumn use.

Cauliflower

Cabbage These embrace a wide variety of different types and include round ones, pointed heads, the little stone-hearted two pounders peculiar to the West Riding of Yorkshire; red ones, half red, crinkly cabbages which are the savoys, coleworts and Chinese cabbages which make an agreeable salad as well as a vegetable.

Few mistakes can be made when growing cabbages, but it must be observed that the varieties listed for spring and summer use are not necessarily suitable for autumn sowing to over-winter.

Some plants notably the cabbage and the onion have within their ranks varieties which are capable of developing as the days are shortening, hence the need for taking care in the selection of varieties.

Cabbages of one sort or another may be had at all seasons of the year. The usual fate, however, is to have a glut at one time of the year until everyone is sick of the sight of them and then none when they are needed. Sowings should be made in July and August for spring use, August in the south and July in the north and the sowings continued from March to July. To maintain a continuous supply, sow thinly and plant out only about a dozen at a time, using round or drumheaded types for summer use and pointed types for spring and autumn use. Plant out at 18in.–24in. spacing, depending on variety.

Treatment as for sprouts—pests and diseases same as all other members of the family.

Foremost and Greyhound are anomg the best for early spring sowing. Primo, a dwarf round-headed. Winnigstadt for late summer and autumn, with January King a very hardy over-wintering type which will stand better than most varieties of savoy especially near large towns where the crinkly savoys get so dirty.

Savoy Cabbage The savoy cabbage is a hardier form well suited for standing as a mature-hearted cabbage through the winter, or late varieties will gradually heart up and can be used as late as March. Treat as for sprouts. It has a greater resistance than summer cabbage to pests and diseases. Tom Thumb is a small-hearted type well suited for small gardens and is very early with Ormskirk at the other end for a very late one.

Red Pickling Cabbage This is grown less than formerly, as for many it is too much trouble to pickle and an often inferior produce is bought instead. This is a pity because this very hardy cabbage can be used as a vegetable in the same way as the green cabbages. This is mentioned because it is thought by some to be poisonous unless salted and soaked in vinegar. Small heads are excellent cut into slices and cooked in ham liquor preferably in a casserole.

This is probably more free of pests and diseases than any of the others mentioned, even caterpillars usually leave it alone.

Mercury or Good King Henry

Is not really a member of the Brassica family but belongs with the spinach and beetroot, but it is so much like the cabbage in habit and in its uses that for convenience it is grouped here.

It is perennial in habit, can be grown from seed sown in April and is planted out about 20 inches apart in well-manured ground and the leaves are pulled as required, but the best parts of this plant are the flower buds which are produced in early spring and taste like asparagus. Do not allow the plants to flower even if you do not wish to use the growths or they will quickly deteriorate. In any case renew the beds every three or four years. Give an annual mulch of manure and an occasional dressing of National Growmore as the better you do for the plant, the better it will do for you.

Kohlrabi

This is a turnip-like vegetable and is too strong in flavour for most palates. They must in any case be eaten young as they become tough and fibrous with age. Use when slightly less in size than a tennis ball.

There is little difference between the two types available—green and purple. Sow seed thinly in early April where they are to crop and thin out to about 6 inches apart. They look like a cross between a turnip and a cabbage and taste about the same and have no great claims as a vegetable.

Couve Tronchuda

A large, loose type of cabbage with prominent wide mid-ribs which are the parts eaten, is also in the same category. Not much point in growing a large spreading plant merely for the sake of the stalk.

Sea Kale

Although a vegetable which has long been grown by the discerning it is seldom seen in the shops and then regarded as a curiosity. Why this should be is a mystery, and fortune awaits the person who could conjure up a method to popularize it. This vegetable is not eaten

49

Cabbage—round

green, although it has a cabbage-like leaf, but the young blanched growths are a delicacy available during the winter months.

It can be grown from seed, but as the plants need to be two years old before they can be blanched, time will be saved if these are brought from the seedsman or nurseryman.

Once a stock is established it is easily propagated by root cuttings which are thong-like growths which can be dug up like horseradish.

The blanching can be done where it is growing by covering with boxes about November. To accelerate growth and keep it warmer, heap leaves or strawy manure around the boxes. In the more spacious days individual sea kale pots with a lid were specially produced, but these are little more than a memory now. The root-like things can also be lifted, planted in pots or boxes of soil, placed in a cellar and covered with inverted pots or empty boxes. The essence of all successful blanching is complete darkness and a gentle warmth to stimulate growth.

Sea kale shares with rhubarb the enviable reputation that it is not attacked by any serious pest or disease and provided it has a good root run, an open situation and an annual dressing of manure, it will go on for all time and provide one of the most delicate and tasty of all vegetables.

It offers almost unlimited methods of cooking, from plain boiling in salted water, to inclusion in meat and cheese dishes.

A dish for the gourmet. *Variety*—Lily White.

Spring cabbage

Carrots   There are several types of this succulent root vegetable which, if used intelligently, will suit almost any type of soil or condition. The most popular types are reddish in colour, but white and cream types were at one time widely grown.

Many people are put off growing carrots because of the ravages and complete destruction of the crop by the grub of the carrot fly. Although large quantities are grown in fields and in some areas do not appear to be unduly affected by carrot fly, it is due in many cases to the open situation of the field where the fly and its larvae (grubs or maggots) are exposed to their natural enemies. There is also a lot of truth in the argument advanced by one of my colleagues who says that where the carrots outnumber the fly you will get carrots, but where the flies outnumber the carrots they will get them.

Actually, the small grower has a better chance of defeating the fly if the job is approached with the idea of forestalling or anticipating the egg-laying female. Although they are barely visible it can be accepted that they can produce two or three broods in a season but rarely after the end of June, so the first control of damage is to sow a short-rooted, early-maturing type, early in July when danger of attack is past.

Although the Short Horn types are excellent for early crops under cloche or early outdoor sowings, they do not produce the weight of crop yielded by the stump-rooted intermediate and long-rooted types.

For the ordinary garden the intermediate varieties are probably the best as they are solid, compact, and do not need such a great depth of soil as the long varieties, besides presenting no difficulty in storing.

Soil for all carrots should be as well worked as possible and completely free from lumps which would cause forking or thonging of the main tap roots. It is often suggested that manure should not be used for carrots, but this applies mainly to large dollops of fresh manure dug into the soil. Where, however, well-rotted compost and manure are available this can be freely dug into the soil. Fairly fine granulated peat is even better still as it allows those very fine hair-like roots which are seldom seen by the gardener to penetrate into the soil.

Before sowing in wide drills as recommended for beetroot, the soil should be well broken with a fork or rotary cultivator.

Sowing can be extended from February to August, using the short horn varieties for early and late work, whilst in March and April, the main crops are sown thinly in rows where they are to mature.

Pests.

It is my belief that the majority of pests which attack plants with strong and unmistakable odours or scents are attracted to these by this characteristic smell. For example, carrot flies or onion flies are worse when the foliage has been disturbed or bruised in the operation of thinning the seedlings. Where this operation of thinning or singling does not take place the crop may easily go through the season without attack, but as soon as carrots or onions are pulled, attacks seem to follow within a few days.

For hundreds of years gardeners have warded off attacks by the egg-laying female by sprinkling sand impregnated with paraffin or naphthalene or by soaking tow with Stockholm tar and laying it along the rows.

One of the drawbacks of these methods which undoubtedly work, is the fact that the materials are not sufficiently absorbent and a heavy shower washes the deterrent out.

Perhaps the best material for deterring these pests is to soak fibrous sedge peat with Jeyes' fluid and work this thoroughly into the soil before sowing the seed and then to scatter it thinly along the rows during the growing season from the time the young plants are about 2 inches high.

Sow the seed thinly at the rate of 1oz. per 100ft. row with the rows spaced at 12 inches apart.

Varieties.

Early Scarlet Horn, Early Short Horn, Early Gem, Early Nantes. Intermediate. Amsterdam Forcing, Chantenay, James' Scarlet. Long: Altrincham Red, St. Valery and Vita Longa.

Carrots under Frames and Cloches.

Carrots are a good cloche crop in that they can be sown nearly two months ahead of those outdoors, which will give them a start so that if cloches or frames are in short supply they can be lifted off the carrots and used over another crop.

Place the cloches over some well-prepared land—that is, soil which has been well broken down with a fork and then raked finely about a fortnight before sowing to allow the soil to warm up.

The number of rows to the cloche will naturally depend on the width of the cloche but generally three can be sown if the cloches are to be lifted before the crop matures. Better results can be had by sowing broadcast over the area to be covered and the seed raked in or lightly covered with sand.

53

Long carrots

If the cloches are placed in position in January a sowing may be made in mid-February using a dwarf variety such as Early Market. Adopt the same procedure for frame culture. To prevent greening of the tops or crowns of the carrots, cover with peat to prevent exposure to sunlight.

Celeriac This vegetable is in effect a turnip-rooted celery, the swollen root of which is eaten instead of the stems as with the celery. It is not, however, as widely known as it should be and seldom finds its way into the shops. The greatest advantage of this vegetable is that the roots can be lifted and stored and be available for use as an ingredient for salad and for flavouring at a time when fresh celery is unobtainable.

The plants are raised from seed sown in a warm greenhouse in sandy soil in March, pricked out in boxes as for celery, hardened off and planted out at about 1ft. apart in early June.

To make a good root the soil should be well-manured and as the bulbous portion of the root sits on the soil, the question of the forking of the roots does not arise as it does with tap-rooted vegetables. In dry seasons celeriac needs plenty of moisture otherwise the roots will be tough and stringy.

Celery

Like celery it develops sucker-like growths from the base and these should be removed so that the swelling root should be kept as clean as possible. Keep free from weeds and as the season advances, about August, draw up a little loose soil around the roots to blanch them.

They may be kept in the ground until late October, or until the tops turn yellow. Then they should be lifted and the roots lightly trimmed and the tops removed and stored in a box of dry sand or ashes.

Celery fly may attack the foliage, but precautionary sprays with Lodane or a B.H.C. spray will take care of this. In country districts a dusting of soot along the rows and on the foliage will not only help prevent attacks of fly, but will stimulate growth as well.

Celery   A vegetable not grown by the home gardener so much as formerly, due perhaps to the fact that it needs a rich soil and to the mistaken notion that much time and labour must be spent on preparing elaborate trenches. A trench is, however, not essential for growing celery; in fact, on shallow soils to plant celery in a trench hewn out of solid clay is to ensure it being a failure. The secret of growing celery is to have as much good rich fertile soil under it as possible and the object of digging a trench was to increase this by putting a layer of manure under it. The trench system also facilitates watering and enabled the old professional gardener to produce a head of celery with several feet of blanched stems.

Digging a trench in clay such as is often found in new gardens, however, is a different proposition entirely from the technique adopted in gardens where fertility had been dug into them for hundreds of years, with the soil many feet deep. Attempts to carry out these old but very admirable techniques often lead to having celery and sweet pea trenches little better than drainage sumps for the whole garden into which the water drains and drowns the roots.

Celery must have moisture, but excess water is more harmful than dryness. In northern gardens and particularly in districts of high rainfall, it would be far better to dig in a little extra manure and plant the celery on the flat instead of excavating.

Where the soil of the garden is a foot or more deep and the trench can be drained if necessary or where it is desired to grow exhibition celery, dig out a trench 18–20 inches wide and one spade deep. Fork' over the bottom and add a good 4 inches of well-rotted manure and return the soil to the trench with the exception of the last 3 inches.

So in effect you have a shallow trench, as one would take out for sowing peas. Remember all the time that the soil piled on the side of a trench is not doing the crop in the trench one scrap of good, the only place soil is any use is under the plants with their roots in it.

It may be asked "what about soil for blanching?" Well this is to hand right alongside the row just in the same way as the soil is alongside a row of potatoes. There is no merit in having a mound of soil between the two rows of celery, in fact it is a nuisance to cultivate and keep clean.

Raising the Plants.
Unless a heated greenhouse or a hotbed is available it is seldom possible for the amateur to raise his own plants which would have a long enough season of growth to produce exhibition heads, but in most parts of the country plants from a March sowing in a cold greenhouse frame, or under cloches, will make good utility heads for the kitchen. Celery plants have masses of fine, fibrous roots— require a light compost in the boxes and as soon as they start growing, an abundance of water.

Because of this vigorous root system the transplanted seedlings or those brought in, will rapidly occupy all the soil space in the boxes and will quickly suffer from being root-bound. This is, how-ever, less liable to happen with late sown seed than with heat-raised plants. To avoid any check to growth with either bought-in plants or early sown ones, it is better to plant them in a cold frame or under cloches at 4 inches apart and then lift them with a good ball of soil to plant out permanently in early June, at 10–12 inches apart in the bed or trench.

Subsequent cultivation consists of keeping the plants growing steadily by giving them water when dry and for this purpose the countryman's practice of pouring washing and bath water along the row is a good one, as this contains salts from the soap which is a mild fertiliser. In dry areas a mulch of manure, peat or even grass mowings will be found beneficial in retaining the moisture in the soil.

As the plants grow it will be found that small sucker-like growths will form at the base of the stalks, these must be removed before any blanching is begun together with any yellowing leaves.

Blanching is done by excluding light and air from the green stems, and can be achieved quite simply by drawing soil around the stems. The easiest way when doing the job single-handed is to tie the stems together with a strand of soft plastic. This has the merit of preventing 57 the soil from falling into the centre and checking growth, and being elastic it will expand as the plant continues to grow. Blanching must be a continuous operation, i.e. if soil is used, 3–4 inches at a time must be drawn up. This has the effect not only of blanching the green stems, but elongates them at the same time. Collars preferably made of tarred paper secured by the same polythene plant tie may be used instead of soil, and in districts where slugs are a pest, "earthing" should be done with sand or peat.

Extra feeding may be given by watering with liquid manure either made from animal or poultry droppings or perhaps better still with a soluble food such as Maxicrop. Never give any food or stimulant while the soil is dry. Soak with clear water first during dry weather.

Good varieties are Wensleydale White, Major Clarke, Red and Champion Pink.

Self-blanching Celery

This is a pale daffodil yellow and if planted in beds with the plants about 8 inches apart, the close planting excluding light from the stems, will need no other aids to blanching. The soil must, however, be very liberally manured or the resultant heads will be tough and leathery. In any case this type will not have the same crispness as the normal earth-blanched types.

It is a complete fallacy to imagine that celery is only fit to eat after being frosted. The action of frost on celery is to kill it, so although frost will sweeten celery in the same way as it does potatoes it means that the tissue is breaking down rapidly and will soon be useless.

Pests and Diseases.
There are certain districts such as the moss and fenlands where the rich organic soils overlay water-soaked peat or organic matter and on these soils the plants grow so well that they are able to throw off many of the attacks of pests or diseases.

In confined gardens where the same traditional skill is not available, would-be growers must get really mad when they read that "Celery fly may be troublesome", and other pests treated as if they were just incidental instead of being devastating.

Celery fly is an insidious pest and once it becomes established it is practically impossible to get rid of as the female deposits her eggs between the upper and lower skins of the leaf. The eggs hatch out and the grub proceeds to feed on the leaf tissue producing an impervious skin much like a plastic and being of dead tissue it cannot absorb insecticide as can living tissue. Certain insecticides such as B.H.C. Benzine Hexachloride is to some extent absorbed by the plant and will control pests such as the larvae of celery fly and leaf mining fly.

A far better control is to coat the leaves of the growing plant with a deterrent or a film of insecticide poisonous to fly and larvae. Such practices as dusting the foliage when wet with soot and lime is an old-established practice to deter the egg-laying female,

Spray regularly with a weak solution of Jeyes' fluid, one teaspoonful per gallon of water, any spray containing B.H.C. or Lodane, which is an emulsified paraffin, or dust the foliage with Derris powder.

Slugs.
Sprinkle Jeypeat along the rows before earthing and pull the soil over this. Afterwards use Slug-it.

Soft Rot.
Is one of the most common causes of crop failures and is due in part to waterlogged trenches and soil in the centre when earthing-up or an excess of wet manure in contact with the roots of the plants.

Deficiency of boron which can be corrected by a minute trace of borax applied at the rate of 1oz. to 10 sq. yds. of soil and to make it easier for distribution mix the borax first with soil or sand.

Chicory

Though used mainly as a salad and eaten uncooked it is a most useful and attractive vegetable which I personally prefer to celery. Much of its attraction is due to its clean, nutty flavour and to the fact that like sea kale, it comes in at a season when there is little else available.

It can be likened to a large dandelion with a long thong-like root and unless blanched thoroughly, is extremely bitter. In fact much of its unpopularity may be due to exposure to light in shop windows prior to purchase, but this can be avoided by the home gardener.

Seeds should be sown in deeply dug but unmanured land in April, an old pea or celery trench is an excellent site for it. Thin out to about 6 inches apart and give one or two light dressings of National Growmore or weak liquid manure during the summer to encourage a strong root system.

Although it should be prevented from flowering when grown for good roots, it is quite an attractive blue flower in the border.

The portion eaten is the cone-shaped tightly compacted bunch of leaves and stem which are produced from the root which is dug up from October onwards for forcing.

Nothing elaborate is needed for forcing as this can be done in a cellar, a large box or even the domestic airing cupboard or in the cupboard usually found under the stairs. A simple way is to dig up half a dozen roots at a time, trim them to 8–9 inches long and plant them in a box vertically with the crowns from which the leaves have been trimmed, flush with the surface of the soil mixture. The soil mixture should be made open with sand and peat and can be used several times. Place a bottomless box of exactly the same size on top of the bottom one and fill with a mixture of peat and sand to about 6–7 inches deep and immediately the "chicons" or points of the growth show through this, it is ready to be cut off from the crown and used. The whole secret of blanching is complete darkness no matter what method is used. There are no diseases or pests to worry about and the best variety is Witloof.

Endive   Endive is a lettuce-like vegetable which shares with chicory a bitter taste if not blanched, but as this is the only job that has to be done to make it different from growing an ordinary lettuce it is surprising that it is not more widely grown. Like chicory, too, it comes into use during the late autumn and winter months when there is no other crisp crunchy salading available. It is even less trouble than chicory as it can be blanched where it is grown, in fact the very crudest method of blanching is to lay a slate or a piece of board on top of the growing plant.

Seeds may be sown in V-shaped drills from early May to early July and a small quantity is best sown at a time to provide a succession of plants for blanching, for when once blanched they should be used within a few days. As it takes about three weeks of darkness to turn a bitter green plant into a creamy crisp salad this will give an indication of the times between sowing. When the seedlings are about 2–3 inches tall thin out to about a foot apart and when the leaves are about 8–10 inches long they are fit for blanching.

They are not entirely hardy in that they will not stand severe freezing, but it is easy to provide protection either by cloches or boards along the row or rows of bricks with glass over the top. In southern districts little trouble should be experienced especially if they are arranged to come into use when the last of the lettuces are finished.

The easiest way to blanch plants is to cover them with a large plant pot, but as they must be in total darkness the hole in the pot must be covered or plugged with a wad of paper.

Few pests or diseases attack endive, but to avoid rotting, cover the plants on a dry day, as wet foliage and the confinement of the plant may set up heart rot.

There are several varieties but the frilly-leaved ones are the most crisp and attractive. French Moss Curled and White Curled are good varieties, Batavian has smooth leaves and is perhaps a bit hardier.

Leeks

The leek is an outstanding vegetable in its own right and should not be regarded as merely a flavouring for soups. In the north it really comes into its own and the mammoth leeks grown for exhibition are as excellent in leek puddings or as a vegetable as they are sources of energy and admiration.

In common with brussels sprouts the leek needs a long season of growth to get really good specimens and no matter how big a leek may be it loses none of its flavour and succulence. Whilst size is not a criterion of flavour, anyone who disparages size in leeks is only crying sour grapes. Confusion often arises as to the difference between "trench leeks" and "pot leeks"; actually there is no difference, it is merely a question as to the method of growing them. True, by constant vegetative reproduction and expert selection, the pot leek has become a characteristic of the northern counties of Durham and Northumberland, but it is just as possible to grow pot leeks in Essex or Surrey as it is in Durham.

The cooler climatic conditions of the northern half of England favour the growth of a vegetable that requires slower, steady conditions of growth. Like every other plant, the better and richer the soil the better the resultant crop will be but provided the soil is not tightly compacted, the large and vigorous root systems will ensure a decent crop even on poor soil.

Propagation.
There are three ways of propagation: seeds, pods and offsets; the last two methods are purely vegetative which means that a part of the parent plant is used so that the resultant plants retain the characteristics of the parent. Thus, if it is desired to perpetuate a characteristic of an excellent strain it can be ensured only by these methods. Such methods have their limitations, so growing each year from seed is the most convenient for most people.

Leeks

The leek is perfectly hardy and has been used as a vegetable from time immemorial and was a staple article of diet in the days of the Pharoahs. Because of its hardiness it can be left in the ground all the winter and used as required.

For earliest crops and for exhibition, seeds should be sown in gentle heat in early January and then pricked out about 2 inches apart in boxes of fairly light soil to produce a good root system. The plants required for exhibition should be potted up into 3-inch pots so that they can grow on without check and be transplanted to the open ground without any damage to the roots.

This business of root damage is particularly important in the case of those members of the lily family such as onions and leeks. These belong to the group of plants which produces only a single seed leaf and are called monocotyledons as distinct from those which produce two seed leaves like the tomato and bean and are called dicotyledons.

In the case of the first group most of them produce roots only from the base of the plant and in the case of onions, leeks and bulbs this comes from a basal plate.

It is most important for the grower to realize this, for if the basal plate is damaged in any way, or roots broken, then there is bound to be a check to growth, hence the advice to pot up or use soil blocks for exhibition specimens.

The main sowings should be made thinly in drills in a seed bed during March and April and when the plants are about 5–6 inches high they should be planted as advised.

Propagation from Pods.
Pods are small growths to be found in the drumstick-like seed head of the leek and look for all the world like germinated seed. On examination a tiny green shoot will be seen emerging from what appears to be a seed which has started to sprout. These are, however, vegetative growths and as such have the virtues of all methods of vegetative methods of propagation in that the true characteristics of the parent plant are faithfully preserved. By seed, this can never be assured. Thus it is of special value to the exhibitor who has bred a particular type and wishes to perpetuate this year after year. In this case it is one of nature's devices to ensure continuity, so if when the seed head falls over naturally and the seeds fail to germinate these embryo plants falling on the soil will be most likely to grow and perpetuate the race. It can thus be seen why the leek is a plant of such great antiquity.

These pods should be removed from the seed head in January and immediately passed gently into a box of light seed compost at about 2 inches apart and treated as young plants straight from the start. Do not remove them on any account before ready for planting as they have little reserve food of their own and depend on that stored in the centre of the seed head to which they are attached.

Grow on as for seedlings.

Offsets.
These will be found springing from the base of the plant and look like small leeks and should be detached and pulled up and sub-

sequently planted out if it is desired particularly to perpetuate a special strain vegetatively.

Soil Preparation.

It is not essential to grow leeks in trenches unless long blanched stems are required; for normal use it is doubtful if this laborious method gives the increased crop when compared with the labour involved. Any good piece of land will do, especially if the crop follows early potatoes, and a good complete fertiliser is lightly forked into the surface at the rate of 2ozs. to the sq. yd. The simplest method of planting is by making holes about 6 inches deep with a blunt-ended dibber and about 6 inches between the holes and from 12 to 15 inches between the rows.

Lift the plants carefully from the seed drills with a hand fork or pointed stick so as not to break the roots and drop them into the holes. All that is necessary is to scrape a small amount of soil merely to cover the roots, but the holes must not be filled in or this will choke the plants.

This filling in will take place during the season as the plants grow and the centre rises above the surface of the ground by ordinary cultural operations such as hoeing. Later in the season the 6-inch length of blanch which is formed in the hole may be lengthened by drawing 3–4 inches of soil around the plants.

Leeks respond to generous feeding either as weak solutions of soluble chemical fertiliser in liquid form, or manure and soot water made by suspending manure and soot in a sack in a tube of water.

As they are surface rooters, do not cultivate too deeply alongside during the summer months, some roots will be destroyed when earthing in late summer, but it is not so vital then as all tissue has been formed by this time and only development, not growth, takes place during the winter months. If the trench method is adopted— prepare the trench and treat as celery.

Leeks need not be lifted from the ground until required for use, but in anticipation of severe weather a few may be lifted and re-planted in a trench near the kitchen door to save trouble if the ground becomes frozen or covered with snow.

Pests and Diseases.

Leeks are such a hardy crop that they do not suffer seriously from any pest but, like onions and shallots, they are sometimes attacked by fungoid diseases.

Pull up diseased plants and change the position for the next crop avoiding the same place for at least three years.

Varieties.
Marble Pillar or Everest can be recommended, whilst for ordinary purposes Musselburgh, Empire, Walton Mammoth and Lyon are good.

Lettuces

This crop is perhaps more of a salad or a vegetable to be eaten raw, but as this applies more or less to all the subjects dealt with it is included here. For example, probably as many peas are eaten raw as are cooked.

Lettuce however, can be cooked as a vegetable. It makes an easily digested soup and supplies all the moisture required if when cooking new garden peas, beans and young carrots a few leaves are put in the bottom of the pan instead of water.

Old plants which have bolted and gone to seed or gone tough at the end of the season are excellent when turned into soups. Two of the biggest mistakes made by unskilled lettuce growers are sowing too many at one time and pricking out the seedlings when they have become too big.

In spite of repeated advice to sow a "pinch" of seed it is a common practice for a lot to be sown at one time with a resultant glut for a week or two and then none for the rest of the year. Small wonder that fantastic prices are charged for inferior heads which are little more than leaves; yet with only a little care and trouble they can be had all the year round.

This happy state does pre-suppose some form of glass protection but even without it they can be had from May till October. The reader will by now either have become bored and tired of the constant reference to a well-prepared soil or has resolved that his shall be in future well prepared. But as this means nothing more than the regular digging at the right time and the addition of manure and fertilisers in anticipation of sowing, no apology is offered for saying that the best, biggest and most succulent lettuces will be harvested from well-drained soil in good heart. Such a soil is especially necessary where plants have to stand the winter outdoors.

Where a greenhouse is available a start may be made by sowing seed in boxes of light soil in a slightly heated greenhouse in January or February and either grown on in beds in the greenhouse or pricked off into boxes to be planted out in a cold frame or under cloches. A technique originated by the author for the small gardener is as follows and may be started in late March or April or in February if cloches are available.

65

Vegetable Garden

Sow a few seeds thinly in a drill half-way across the garden plot using a utility variety such as All the Year Round. When the plants are about an inch high, thin them out to 4 inches apart, removing the unwanted plants by lifting them carefully with a label or a pointed stick. Use as many of these plants as are necessary to plant up the remainder of the row again at 4 inches apart discarding the remainder of the seedlings unless the rows are less than 10 ft. (20 ft. in all) when another row can be planted with them. The thinned out seedlings will be ready for use some two to three weeks before the transplanted ones and both these and the seedlings left at 4 inches apart can have every alternate plant taken out and used when half-grown leaving the others at 8 inches to develop fully. Treat the transplanted plants in the same way, that is, use up each alternate one when half-grown.

When the first lot is nearly used up sow another half row in the same way and repeat until the end of June when it will be too late to transplant. After this date and up to the end of July, sow where they are to mature.

Lettuces are so easy to grow that anyone can be successful if it is remembered to transplant early—not more than 2 inches high.

Varieties are numerous and have been highly developed to meet special needs and to mature under different conditions and temperatures and anyone contemplating growing these for a sideline would do well to study the many varieties offered. Cos Lettuce, a tall, narrow leafed variety, is better grown in the southern half of the country.

One of the biggest pests is root aphis which are greyish aphides which infest the roots and may kill the crop. They are especially troublesome during dry weather and soaking each plant with water to which a B.H.C. insecticide is added will keep them in check.

Onion—White Portugal

Good varieties are—Cabbage varieties: All the Year Round, Arctic King, Continuity, Cheshunt Early Giant, Hilde, and Webbs Wonderful. Tom Thumb hearts a little later than all of these but is ideal for the small garden. Cos varieties: Buttercrunch, Balloon, Little Gem (formerly known as Sugar Cos), Paris White and Winter Density.

Onions

Perhaps a flavouring which is missed more than any other is that of the onion; in fact, many readers will recall to what lengths people went to obtain even a suggestion of onion flavour during the Second World War.

So much has been written about onions that the impression is deeply rooted that only an expert can grow onions successfully. If by this is meant $4\frac{1}{2}$–5lb. bulbs, then it is true, but these are the aristocrats of the onion world and something much smaller is of more use to the housewife.

Usable and even large onions may be grown either from seed or from "sets". Sets are small onions which have been specially grown from seed, usually in hot climates, so that they make a small ripe bulb about the size of a nutmeg so that when planted in cooler, moister conditions they will grow and increase in size.

Their behaviour, however, is very erratic, so much so that there is no guarantee that they will do what is expected of them, sometimes producing reasonable crops and at other times running quickly to seed. They have this merit in that they are seldom attacked by the onion fly which may decimate a crop grown from seed.

Propagation.

The best plants are raised from seed sown in boxes of light soil in January in a warm greenhouse. Prick out seedlings 2 inches apart when 2 inches high and grow on steadily in a temperature around 50°F. (10°C.). Later they are placed in a cold frame and then hardened off by increasing ventilation and finally planted out in well prepared soil in April.

Onions must have a good rich soil and will not grow successfully on the soil of a new garden or in soil which has been tipped on to a garden site. In fact, on such soils, it may be five years before really large onions can be grown. They are, too, plants of environment in that the would-be exhibitor will be successful if he saves his own seed from selected bulbs. In fact, up to three pounds may be added in about four years if own seed is saved. Suppose that an exhibitor

68

wishes to set out to beat the board he should start off by obtaining seed of the best possible strain. All reputable seed firms can supply these and for the uninitiated these will be at the beginning of the onion list described as so and so's Exhibition.

Start off from this point and grow on as will be described, and at the end of the season select the best shaped bulbs with thin necks, having all the characteristics desired. Keep the bulb or bulbs in a dry, cool place until January and then pot these up in 10-inch plant pots by pressing the base into the soil in the pot. Water and grow as an ordinary plant in a cool greenhouse or frame, stand outdoors in April and plunge the pot partly into the soil to prevent it being blown over. When the flower spike is formed, stake and tie it to a bamboo cane as it is very brittle and may be broken in a strong wind: don't be deceived by its apparent strength.

The actual time of ripening will depend on district, and this is one reason why potting is advised. In a cold, wet summer or in northern districts the pot may be carried under shelter and the ripening seed ensured.

In districts where competition is very keen, rivals have been known not infrequently to harvest each other's seed, so a pot can be put safely under lock and key.

This process should be repeated annually—one great grower has done this careful saving and re-selection for nearly forty years and possesses probably the best strain in the world. In my opinion this is the only way to be sure of getting really fine onions every year.

Strain in all plants is very important so be sure to start off right.

Soil preparation.
Whilst it is important to have a good fertile soil, it is of the utmost importance to have a well-worked and a well-drained one. This does not mean that an elaborate system of drains is necessary, but that the bottom spit or layer of soil be broken up with a fork and a quantity of rough material such as compost, peat, strawy manure of even hedge clippings and chrysanthemum stalks be worked into this bottom layer. The treatment will vary according to the nature of the soil, but as onions prefer a medium heavy soil the object of putting opening material underneath will be to assist and if it is light soil this material will help to absorb and retain moisture.

Prepare the soil during October and November so that it has a chance to settle down before planting. This firming of the soil is important but it must not be taken to apply to every soil, only light spongy soils need hard treading or rolling, most soils need nothing more than the walking on necessary when raking it down.   69

Onion var. Ailsa Craig

After the initial double digging it may not be necessary to do this again for many years so long as no waterlogging takes place. Add to the soil when digging each year, 2ozs. bonemeal and 2–3ozs. of muriate of potash per sq. yd. in addition to a good heaped barrow load of manure to each 6 sq. yds.

In March break down the roughly dug soil with a fork and add 3ozs. of superphosphate before forking. Then dust the surface lightly with hydrated lime. Leave for another week then firm and rake the surface over with a wide-toothed wooden rake before planting.

Whether planting your own raised plants or those bought in from a nurseryman, do not leave the roots exposed by laying the plants along the row preparatory to planting, but keep them covered with a wet cloth.

Do not plant deeply but try to place the basal plate from which the roots emerge about an inch below the soil. At all times plant out with a trowel and make a hole deep enough so that roots are not cramped or broken.

Size and quantity of crop are comparative and one person may be well satisfied with results that another would scorn as inferior, but if best results are to be obtained consistently year in and year out, then every attention must be paid to detail. Unless the crop shows signs of disease or severe pest infestation the same bed may be used every year when it will increase in fertility.

Not everyone, however, will require huge onions for exhibition. The easiest and most rewarding way of growing them for the kitchen is to sow seeds thinly in a wide shallow drill as advised for beetroot, using a variety like Ebenezer. In this way no thinning is either necessary or desirable, but it is essential to sow thinly and a little extra time should be spent in seeing that the seeds fall about 2 inches apart. Onion seeds are quite big and as by this method no other operation is needed such as thinning or transplanting, the little extra time is worth the bother. In fact, with any of these wide drill techniques a bucketful of special compost can be made up from ordinary garden soil from the plot and mixed with equal parts sand and granulated peat to cover the seed.

If the soil is dry, water the drill before sowing, never after covering. When grown in this way do not pull the young plants to eat as "Scallions" or spring onions for salad, but sow a row especially for this purpose as far away from the main crop as possible.

No attention is necessary except to keep the row free from weeds and allow the bulbs to ripen where they are grown, these will be hard, well flavoured long-keeping bulbs about the size of a small orange, a most useful size for the kitchen.

Autumn-sown Onions.
Sowing seeds in late summer is only a variation of early spring sowing and the resultant seedlings can either be planted out in beds or pulled from the drills as salading. It is important, however, to select the correct variety for as in common with most other plants it is the nature of the beast to stop growing and ripen as the days shorten and the temperature drops, but certain varieties of onions and brassica not only germinate but grow during the ever shortening days of winter.

For example, such varieties as Ailsa Craig, Bedfordshire Champion, Lancastrian and Reliance can be used for both spring and autumn sowing, with White Lisbon for pulling green for salads and The Queen is a small early silver-skinned variety for pickling.

Onions for Salads.
No large quantity of these should be sown at any one time and as they remain where they are sown a pinch can be sown at any time starting in late summer or autumn and continued in spring. The variety White Lisbon is a mild, hardy type and is widely used for this purpose, a single row sown between a row of peas is an ideal spot for them.

The less the soil on an onion bed is disturbed the better and hand-weeding should be done instead of doing too much hoeing as this loosens up the surface soil and makes it easier for the female onion fly to lay her eggs near the plants.

If the young plants do not seem to be getting away as they should, give them a tonic of 1oz. potash nitrate to a gallon of water—about a pint to each plant. This may be continued at monthly intervals until August, or weak liquid manure may be given instead, but if the soil has been well prepared as advised, little extra feed need be given. To help the bulbs ripen give an application of superphosphates about a teaspoonful to each plant in early August.

If they have been planted correctly it will not be found necessary to scrape soil away from the base of the bulb except when well-ripened bulbs are required for exhibition when an evenly browned skin counts.

Little if any benefit is secured by bending over the tops in an effort to assist ripening. If the necks are thin and the bulbs nicely ripening they will fall over of their own accord, but even if thick-necked bulbs are bent over it will not make them into good ones. Such bulbs will not store well so use these first.

Harvest by easing up with a fork—bulbs which have completed their growth will part easily from the soil. Spread the bulbs on sacks and expose to as much sun and air as possible to complete the ripening process and tie in bunches after a few days and hang in a cool frost-proof shed.

Onion Sets.
In many districts adverse conditions sometimes make it almost impossible to obtain a good crop of onions from seed. The use of onion sets solves this problem. For these the treatment is simple, the

soil is prepared as for sowing seeds, planting the sets shallowly from mid March onwards. Allow 4 to 6 inches between the bulbs with 12 to 15 inches from row to row. Sets are much less liable to run to seed in a dry season than seed raised plants.

Onion Pests and Diseases.
The onion is not subject to many diseases but may be attacked by a fungus which shows as a white mould. This is more prevalent in wet seasons and where an excess of nitrogenous fertilisers has been used. Pull up the affected plants and burn, dust the area and adjacent plants with a mixture of equal parts hydrated lime and flowers of sulphur and shift the bed to another part of the garden.

Pests.
Of these the onion fly is the most serious and here again it will be found that a deterrent such as paraffin, Jeyes or naphthalene will give better results than trying to effect a cure after an attack.

It may be thought old-fashioned to use such methods nowadays but they have the merit of cheapness and are effective.

Alternatively, the rows can be dressed with 4 per cent Calamel dust.

Parsley

Parsley with its attractive crinkly leaves is well-known and used for garnishing and for sauce, but is little used nowadays as a tonic. As it can be dried in a slow oven to retain its colour, it can be had for all purposes at any time of the year if stored in a dry, cool place after drying.

The most ancient of all garden writers wrote: "Parsley loveth the shade" and this is as true today as when it was written thousands of years ago; but not the shade of dripping trees.

Seed is very slow in germinating so should be sown when the soil is warming up in April and although the young plants can be transplanted, like all tap rooted subjects they make better plants in most cases if the seed is sown thinly and the resultant plants thinned out to about 10–12 inches apart.

The place for parsley is alongside the garden path as not only does it make an attractive edging, but is conveniently placed in all weathers to gather the few odd leaves required.

Although old plants will continue production for several years a second sowing is best made in July or August to stand the winter. In some districts it may be necessary to protect the plants by covering with cloches or by planting a few plants in a cold frame to provide

Parsnips

fresh leaves during the winter months. The richer the soil the better the leaves, but parsley succeeds in almost any soil. Harvest by cutting off the leaves in August and dry on paper in a cooking oven, do not cut hard from plants intended to provide fresh leaves for winter use. Remove old coarse leaves when no longer fit for use and destroy any slugs found hiding there.

Pests and Diseases.
There are few, but in dry seasons it may suffer from root aphis; copious watering will reduce this risk. It may be attacked by the same leaf mining maggot which affects parsnips and celery so avoid

growing it close to these plants. As the leaf is the portion used it is not advised to spray with anything strong smelling as a preventative. Triple curled and Myatt's Garnishing are two good varieties.

This is a dual purpose vegetable, the roots being used like parsnips and the tops as parsley. Seed is sown in deeply cultivated ground in early April, making the rows $\frac{1}{4}$ inch deep and 15 inches apart. Thin out seedlings so they stand 9 inches apart.

Parsley Hamburg

Pea—Early Onward

The roots about 6 or 7 inches long will be ready for use from October onwards. They are hardy and can be used as required, or taken up and stored in boxes of moist sand.

Parsnips

This vegetable is not everybody's cup of tea, but if instead of just "plain boiled" as a vegetable the cook should cut it into chip-like pieces, parboil in salted water, dry and then drop into hot fat and fry till brown, more parsnips would be grown. Alternatively, bake and cover with butter.

Parsnips will not transplant so the seeds must be sown where they are to grow; the best way is to sow the seeds in a V-shaped drill in groups of three at about 8 inches apart with 18–20 inches between the rows. The seeds are very light and look like oatmeal, so avoid sowing on a breezy day.

Germination is slow, partly because the seed is normally sown from February and partly by reason of its nature and habit. The largest and longest roots result from the earlier sowing, but for the housewife who prefers a short stumpy root April sowing is early enough.

The soil must be free from large clods or new manure as the roots quickly fork and instead of a large tapered root it becomes a mass of thongs, so the soil which has been dug over in autumn must be well broken down with a fork and not merely raked over.

As the seed is slow in germinating it is quite possible that masses of small weeds may spring up and obscure the line of the row, making it difficult to hoe between the rows and hand-weed the crop. To overcome this make a thin line of hydrated lime over the top of the covered drill or, alternatively, sow a few lettuce seeds along the drills with the parsnip seed, these will germinate first and row cultivation can take place with no risk of damage to the seedlings. When about 3 inches high, thin the seedling groups to one plant. Subsequent cultivation merely consists of keeping them free from weeds.

For exhibition, special stations should be prepared, a method which can be used for carrots as well and consists of containers such as large boxes, drums or drainpipes filled with good soil sifted through a half-inch sieve, 7 parts, to which has been added 2 parts granulated peat and 1 part well-rotted manure, with a 3-inch potful of a well balanced organic fertiliser. Ordinary garden soil may, of course, be used and where a fair number of specimens are required the effect of a bottomless box can be achieved by making a trough-like box with two boards or other supports. A tapered hole made with a crowbar wiggled round in the ground and filled with prepared soil is often recommended, but this is only possible on medium to light soils. If, however, this is done on heavy soils, the pressure will make a funnel into which water will run and the result will be anything but a specimen root. Far better to make 6-inch holes about 18 inches deep with a draining spade or a trowel and fill in with specially prepared soil.

Pests and Diseases.
Few pests attack parsnips, perhaps the most serious being a leaf mining fly, but if they are sprayed at the first sign of attack with an insecticide containing B.H.C., it will control them.

The worst disease is rusty-looking fungus which mostly attacks the top portion. This is generally a secondary disease which follows even slight damage. As the parsnip is very soft and spongy even a small crack will be sufficient to allow of entry. This disease is more of a disfigurement than a really damaging one, but makes the roots unusable for exhibition.

An easy control is to cover the crowns with peat as soon as they are about the thickness of a thumb, better still use peat impregnated with Jeyes' fluid at the rate of 10ozs. to a bucketful of peat. Repeat this at intervals during the growing season.

Peas

The garden pea has long been valued as an edible crop. They are grouped as either round or wrinkled, the former being hardier and widely used for autumn sowing. The wrinkled varieties are of superior flavour but not always as heavy cropping.

Peas succeed in medium loam with a fairly high water table and an adequate lime content. By careful planning it is possible to have a supply of fresh peas from the garden from mid-May to mid-October. Cloches are a help in obtaining the earliest pickings and they will also be useful for covering the late sowing.

The autum sowing should be grown on fairly light soil which has been well prepared and enriched with organic matter. Avoid fresh manure since this leads to coarse growth and fewer pods. Once the soil has been worked into a fine, friable condition, flat bottomed or V-shaped drills should be drawn out 3 inches deep. Distance apart depends on variety, but as a guide dwarf sorts growing 12 to 15 inches high should be spaced 15 inches apart and those 2 to 3 feet high should be allowed up to 3 feet between rows.

The earliest sowings are made more thickly than those in the spring, and $\frac{3}{4}$ pint of seed will sow a row 50 feet long, whereas only $\frac{1}{2}$ pint is

77

needed for the later sowings. Twiggy sticks should be inserted along the rows as soon as the seedlings can be seen. This applies to all varieties since it protects the seedlings from wind damage and falling over to become a prey to soil pests. Suitable supports should be given as growth proceeds.

Varieties.
First Earlies, round seeded—Meteor 1½ ft.; Pilot 1½ ft.; and Laxton's Superb 2 ft. First Early, wrinkled—Gradus 3 ft.; Kelvedon Wonder 15 in.; Little Marvel 1½ ft.; Early Onward 2 ft. Second Early—Phenomenon 2 ft.; Onward, 2 ft.; Green Shaft 2– 2½ft. Maincrop—Histon Kingsize 3½ ft; Lord Chancellor 3–4 ft., and Senator 3 ft.

There are several different types of peas which are of value in the kitchen including the so-called Sugar Peas. Of these, Petit Pois 3 ft. is the true small seeded French pea. Sweet Green 1½ ft. is another Sugar Pea which is a heavy cropper and both of these should be cooked whole while small, as is the case with the Asparagus pea, which grows only 12 inches.

Salsify

Salsify is a tap rooted vegetable not widely grown, partly because it is not a heavy cropper and to some the flavour is insipid, but cooked in the old-fashioned way, that is, lightly scraped then steeped in vinegar, then boiled, then fried in butter, it is truly a delicacy. Unfortunately, few housewives have time to bother with such a vegetable nowadays.

Sow seed in early April in soil which must be thoroughly broken down and have received no fresh manure as they easily fork and become useless. Dig for use when about as thick as the thumb or they may be left in the ground through the winter like parsnips or dug and stored in sand.

No pests nor diseases.

Scorzonera

Very much like salsify in appearance and in cultivation, except that the skin is black. The flesh, however, is white. Like all tap rooted vegetables it must have a deep, well-worked soil and is really a vegetable for the lighter soils as it so easily forks.

Treat as for salsify.

Shallots

This multi-bulbed, onion-like crop is not so widely grown, being

New Zealand Spinach

superseded by the larger onion and in this age of hurry the cook rarely has time to either pickle or use them for flavouring. In soups they are excellent cooked whole and have a distinctive flavour. Curiously enough they are still very popular at shows where there are now two classes, one for the large, almost onion-like variety and another for the smaller pickling type.

They do not, however, like a heavily manured soil when planted, but are better fed during the growing season if large bulbs are required. Shallots may be grown from small bulbs saved from the

79

preceding year or from seed. Bulbs must not, however, be saved from a crop grown from seed as nearly all will go to seed without making a decent bulb cluster. They are very hardy and may be planted in January or early February in a well-worked soil in rows 12–15 inches apart with the bulbs about 9 inches apart in the rows.

For very large bulbs draw up a low ridge about 3 inches high. Do this from each side so that there is a slight depression in the top into which the bulbs can be lightly pressed.

Apart from their use as dry bulbs the shallot makes an excellent salading and for an early supply of these spring onion-like growths a small quantity of bulbs may be planted in November. Plant these at half the above distances.

For ordinary crops plant by making a little hole with a pointed stick and insert the base in this, for if they are pressed into heavy soil the cup so formed will become hard so that when the roots sprout, the bulbs will be forced out of the ground.

Sparrows sometimes peck at the green tips and pull them out, but as the roots are very brittle they should not be pressed back as this will break them. Replant with a trowel to about half the depth of the bulb.

During the summer keep the crops free from weeds and when the tops have ripened and begun to turn brown, the clusters or cloves should be eased up with a fork and dried on sacks on a hard surface.

Store by putting in nets or wire baskets and hang in a cool, airy place where under good conditions they will last for up to two years.

Pests and diseases.
No pests attack shallots except in extreme cases when slugs in wet districts will attack the loose skin and so encouraged may devour all the bulb.

Spinach This vegetable is too often regarded as something which is good for you and whether it is agreeable is another matter. Here again cooking plays a big part as to whether the family eats it as a nice vegetable and enjoys it or just because of its medicinal and tonic properties. Cooked slowly on a low light with no water or salt, served with plenty of butter, it graces any meal.

There are several varieties but the Silver or sea kale beet (*Lucullus*) is far superior and should not be confused with spinach beet. When well grown sea kale beet is a noble vegetable with broad green leaves and a midrib 4–6 inches wide and 1 foot long. The green leaf can be stripped from this and used as a spinach. The stem can be cut and

80

divided into strips and cooked as a vegetable, used raw as a salad or as a delightful pickle.

Boiled, strained and packed into jars and covered with vinegar it will keep for months and tastes like samphire. The gourmet will already know that samphire is a succulent growth gathered on salt marshes and found along the Lincoln and Norfolk coasts as well as along the Wirral and is a rare delicacy hard to come by. Anyone fond of sea food will assuredly be fascinated with this delightful way of serving it.

It has the further merit that leaves can be gathered in most districts throughout the year and in difficult and cold districts the protection of a few plants with cloches will ensure supplies of this most useful vegetable even during the winter.

The seeds, which may be sown from April to July, resemble beet seeds and the resultant plants should be thinned out to a foot apart when 2–3 inches high. Thin out to about 4 inches apart at the first thinning so that at the next thinning the plants may be used whole as a tasty vegetable. Make a later sowing at the end of July to provide plants to stand the winter, but as these will not grow so large, thin out only to 6 inches apart for their final thinning and do not feed or they will become too soft.

Like the beet this is a maritime plant and enjoys a dressing of common salt, 2ozs. per yard run.

The richer the soil, the better the plant, but reasonable crops can be grown in any soil from sand to stiff clay.

For large exhibition plants with a 6-inch white midrib which will sweep the board in a class for "Any other Vegetable" give occasional feeds with weak liquid manure or potash nitrate at 1oz. to a gallon. Neither sulphate of ammonia nor nitrate of soda should be applied closer than about ten days before gathering the leaves as this tends to make the flavour strong.

It is a matter of choice as to whether the whole plant is cut or whether a few leaves be picked from each plant, but a sound rule is to cut the whole plant of the April crop and to gather odd leaves from the July sown plants.

Pests and Diseases.
About the only pest likely to attack spinach is the black fly of the same ilk that attacks broad beans, but if the colonies which first appear on the undersides of the leaves are sprayed with an insecticide as soon as they are first noticed, it can soon be controlled. There are no diseases that seriously trouble sea kale beet and there are no separate varieties to worry about.

Potato—var. Catriona

Other forms of spinach are the Prickly and Round leaved but for the home gardener they are far inferior; their cultivation is the same as for sea kale beet.

New Zealand is a prostrate type and is better grown for green manuring than for eating. but may be useful on very dry sandy soils. Spinach is very prone to run to seed during a dry season but sea kale beet even if it does run up to seed can be used to the last leaf without detracting from its value.

Potatoes No other food crop has had such a profound influence on the economic history of the world and even in our age of rapid transport of foodstuffs from every corner of the world, few main meals are served without potatoes in some form or another.

At various places in the book it has been stressed that although no-one who has the wherewithal to buy anything, need go without vegetables, but vegetables sold in shops and on market stalls must inevitably lose much of their freshness and flavour in transport and in store. Deep freeze storage retains more nearly the true flavour than any other method. Another aspect of this matter of taste and flavour which makes or mars a vegetable dish is that this is only incidental to the large commercial grower. His aim is to grow bulk producing varieties which will travel well and look well when displayed. Naturally, of course, when a crop has all these attributes he will willingly grow them. But as an illustration take two varieties of potato, Golden Wonder and Majestic. Golden Wonder is a quality potato by any standard, but it produces a crop less than half the tonnage produced by a similar area planted with Majestic. Majestic is a sound, large potato of reasonable quality and for economic reasons the farmer must produce a weighty crop to enable him to make a profit. The home gardener on the other hand is not bound by these limitations and he can afford in most cases to put quality first, with bulk as a secondary consideration. Therefore, it should be his first consideration to select varieties which will have the greatest appeal when cooked.

The potato is very accommodating and will grow in any soil and under all but waterlogged conditions, but grows to perfection in certain areas such as Yorkshire and Lincolnshire where the soil is deep and fertile. Reproduction is by tubers planted in the ground and although the correct name for these tubers is "setts" they are more generally referred to as "seed", a term which will be used hereafter for convenience and in accordance with common usage.

Although it is possible and practicable for a gardener to save seed from his own crop year after year, it has been found that better results are obtained if seed from another area is used after about three years' growing on the same site. There are, of course, exceptions to this, but this is a general practice.

Seed grown in Scotland is generally accepted as the best, not that it will always produce the heavier crop. In fact, once grown Scotch seed invariably produces the heavier yield. The main reason for using Scotch seed is that it is freer from risk of disease due in part to a cooler climate and that greenfly is not so troublesome as a distributor of disease. Seed from other countries such as Ireland and the Isle of Man is also excellent and from other areas such as Lincolnshire, but these are better once grown. If own seed is saved it should be of moderate size, roughly about the size of a hen's egg and should be selected as each root is dug. The reason for this is that certain diseases such as leaf curl will result in all the tubers being of a small, even size; in fact, just the sort likely to be picked out for seed if all the tubers are collected into one heap and then graded. Commercial growers of seed are, of course, aware of this and their fields are rigorously examined during the growing season and any plants showing any signs of disease or variation in type are promptly destroyed.

These precautions are responsible for the higher price of seed as compared to "Ware" potatoes bought at the greengrocers. A question often arises about the size of seed potatoes as to whether large potatoes are better than medium-sized tubers. Actually, there is nothing in it from the cropping point of view but obviously to use large tubers would be much more expensive owing to their greater weight. This can, of course, be overcome by cutting the tubers, but it is essential that each portion should have one or more "eyes"; an ideal number would be three. The cutting is best done not more than a few hours before planting. It is not now regarded as necessary to dust the cut surface with lime or sulphur, but it must not be allowed to become dry.

Chitting.

This widely adopted practice is the setting up of the tubers in shallow boxes with the eye or "rose" end uppermost in a frostproof green-house or other light place. Doing this does materially increase the crop yield and also enables the grower to reduce the number of sprouts or remove any weak ones. The more the seed is exposed to light and air the better and the home gardener can do this as soon as they are lifted, as early greening assists in keeping them through the winter and the housewife is not then liable to use the carefully saved seed tubers; an accident which often happens even in the best of households.

When assessing the quantity of seed required it can be reckoned that approximately 12lbs. of potatoes will be needed for 100 feet of row, with an average yield of between 100–150 lbs. per 100 feet.

Potatoes are grouped according to their times of maturing: Earlies, Second Earlies, Maincrop or Late, but for practical purposes Earlies and Maincrop are of the greatest importance. It being the general practice to grow Earlies for eating "new" or immature, and to allow the maincrop to ripen and be stored for winter use.

The planting distances given below are approximate and based on established practice.

Depth of planting 4–6 inches.

Distance between plants		*Distance between rows*	
Early varieties	9 inches	Earlies	18 inches
Second Earlies	12–15 inches	Second Earlies	24 inches
Maincrop	16–20 inches	Maincrop	30 inches

Planting dates will vary slightly, but in general they may be regarded as extending from early April until the end of May, commencing with the earlies

The potato is an accommodating crop and provided the sett is under the soil it will grow. There are, however, three main methods of planting: by dibber, in trenches and lazy bed.

Place a garden line in position across a piece of well dug and manured ground and make holes with a blunt-ended dibber, on which the depth can be indicated by driving a small nail. The tuber is then dropped shoot end upwards into the hole which is filled with loose soil. This method is only suggested for very well-worked garden soils or a very light soil.

Planting in a trench which simulates ploughing, has the advantage that the soil may be dug, manure added and planted in one operation. When this method is used it can be reckoned that a row of potatoes can be planted at every third row. Measure out the appropriate distance from the preceding row, put down a garden line, place the blade of the spade against the line, press in and pull the soil towards you, making a trench with a straight, clean cut back about 10 inches deep.

Into this put farmyard manure, compost or other organic matter such as fish manure. Cover this lightly with soil so that it brings the layer to within 5–6 inches from the normal surface of the garden. Place the potatoes on this and cover by digging the next spit forward. If there is any doubt about the fertility of the soil, scatter a handful of a complete fertiliser such as National Growmore along the drill or trench, but avoid sprinkling it on the actual tuber.

Take care when planting to avoid breaking off the brittle shoots from the sett and if by any chance they have become fairly long, which would bring them too near the surface, do not bury the tuber deeper but lay it on its side. If when planted, the tips of the shoots are closer than 4 inches to the surface they can easily be damaged by late frosts.

Take care to mark at least the end and beginning of the rows with a stick or label and if the garden is very weedy, it may be advisable to hoe the surface before the potatoes show through the ground. Thus if each row is marked with a stick a line can be placed between the sticks and the space between hoed without risk of damaging the plants.

Lazy Bed Method.
This is an excellent method to adopt on thin soils, i.e. a thin layer of good soil overlying clay or rocky shale. In this case the potatoes are actually laid on the surface of the ground and soil is drawn over them with a hoe or spade from each side so that they are covered with an inverted V-shaped ridge of soil to a depth of about 6 inches. Fertiliser can be dusted along the rows in the same manner as in the trench.

The potato is very tender and liable to frost damage, so avoid low lying land for early crops. As a further precaution draw loose soil completely over the young growths when frost threatens in early spring. Such conditions likely to produce late frosts are clear night skies following a sunny day. The more finely the soil is cultivated between the rows the better, as it is into this fine soil that the underground stems of the potato extend and on which are borne the new potatoes.

Earthing Up.
Earthing or the drawing of soil from each side of the row into a ridge about a foot high has shown that it does not increase the yield per plant, but as it has several advantages it is worthwhile continuing this practice. Two of the most important reasons are that as the stem or haulm of the potato is hollow it is easily broken by wind or rain, and if this is damaged, the flow of sap is restricted and growth is slowed up. Earthing up prevents the tubers nearest the surface from becoming greened and useless from exposure to the sun, but if no earthing is done this can be overcome by spreading straw alongside the rows. The ridge also acts as a protection against disease spores being washed down to the tubers from the leaves by heavy rain.

In some districts it is the practice to earth up twice, once when the tops are about a foot high followed by a further ridging about a month later, but for all practical purposes one is sufficient.

It is a good practice to scatter a special potato fertiliser or National Growmore along the rows before drawing the earth over it at the rate of a handful per running yard on each side of the row. To prevent the ravages of slugs, scatter Jeypeat—peat impregnated with Jeyes' fluid—along the rows at the same time and draw earth over this, too.

Lifting the Crop.
There is no golden rule to decide when to lift a crop for use and no
dates can be given because of the difference in season, variety and
variability of soil. The most satisfactory method is simply to scrabble
into the soil and explore with the fingers before lifting an experimental root. As the first new potatoes of the season are a real treat,
those ranging in size from a walnut to a bantam's egg will warrant
"a boiling".

Sweet Corn var. Kelvedon Glory

This applies to the early varieties for as far as the maincrop is concerned, they may be left until the tops begin to die down and lifting an experimental root will show if the skins have become firm. If lifted too early the skin will become raggy and the tubers will go soft in store. October is the usual month, but in north-western districts where keel slugs are troublesome and they have not been protected with Jeypeat, lift not later than the first week in September or the crop may be a total loss. In these areas it is better to stick to the growing of early varieties such as Arran Pilot, Sharpes Express and Home Guard. Sharpes Express although an early variety will keep very well and will not lose in quality in store.

When lifting for storing save any seed required from the heaviest yielding roots and leave all the tubers exposed to the air for an hour or two before putting into store. This hardens the skins and makes them less liable to damage.

Although farm produced potatoes have to put up with a lot of banging about this can be avoided in the home garden and if picked up into a bucket first they should be put in carefully and emptied as gently as possible.

It is rather silly to take great care of a crop when growing and then to damage it before storing.

Lift with a potato fork if possible, this is a flat-tined fork specially designed for the job and if the haulm has not died down, a possibility during a cool, damp season, cut it off about 6 inches above the ground with a sickle or a pair of shears. Insert the fork between the plants and lift with a forward shovelling motion, pick over at the same time throwing two rows to one single row to facilitate subsequent picking up. When picking up try to do this each day so that none are left out in case it rains. If wetted by rain, although the top quickly dries, the underside of the tuber in contact with the wet soil will remain wet unless turned over and the drier the tubers are when put into store the better they will keep.

Clamping.

Potatoes will keep in clamps which are mounds of soil first covered with straw and subsequently with a thick layer of soil. This is less widely practiced now than formerly, as it is becoming more general for the home gardener to grow varieties which he can enjoy straight from the ground and enough to see the household through until Christmas, relying on farm grown crops for winter use.

To make a clamp, be it for carrots, beetroot, potatoes, apples or dahlia tubers, all of which can be stored in this way, select a piece of well-drained ground at the highest point of the garden and cover with a foot of dry straw. Tip the potatoes on this in a conical heap and cover with another thick layer of straw, then dig a wide trench round the clamp throwing the soil on the straw and firm down with the back of the spade. Leave a wisp of straw protruding from the top of the cone for about a fortnight to take care of any sweating, then cover with soil.

Potatoes may also be stored in boxes, barrels, tea chests and even sacks. These, however, should be placed on a little wooden platform raised from the floor so that air can circulate underneath. Avoid a bright light and try to maintain an even temperature of around 40°–45°F. Anything warmer will excite stored vegetables into growth and shrivelling will take place. Potatoes once frozen will quickly rot.

Pests and Diseases.
These are legion, but a whole list would be depressing and would be as long almost as the ills that could beset mankind. From our own experience, however, we know that no-one gets all the possible ailments and diseases all at once. So with potatoes and if a few common-sense precautions are taken one may go a whole lifetime without serious trouble.

Of the pests underground, keel slugs and wireworms do the most damage. For protection against slugs the ground may be treated when dug over with 1lb. powdered copper sulphate with 7lbs. hydrated lime mixed intimately in with the soil at least three weeks before planting. With this treatment it is not the quantity used, but the least amount mixed thoroughly into the soil that matters, as neither of these elements are good for the crop. Treat at planting and at earthing-up time with Jeypeat as advised. Wireworms and milli-pedes can do great damage on new land especially in gardens attached to new houses, the land of which was formerly pasture or badly neglected. As a precaution use a fertiliser such as Vegerite or Maxi-crop.

Fortunately colorado beetle is rare in this country, but if a beetle about $\frac{1}{3}$ of an inch long is noticed with a yellow body and black stripes or pinkish grubs are seen feeding on the foliage, report to the police who will advise you whom to notify.

As far as diseases are concerned, perhaps the most serious is blight and follows as a rule damp, warm, muggy conditions from June to July. The home gardener seldom has the equipment to do the necessary spraying with Burgundy or Bordeaux mixture, but if you hear on the radio or read in the papers about outbreaks, excellent protection can be given by drenching with a fine-rosed watering can or by dusting with a fungicidal powder. Fortunately, this disease seldom attacks crops in or near industrial towns, but if it should be necessary to spray, the fungicide should be used at half strength or scorching will result due to excess sulphur already in the air.

In some gardens the crop is often badly disfigured by a surface scab; this, however, is mainly a disfiguring disease and is accentuated by adding lime or ashes to the soil. Exhibitors who want their tubers to be as clean as possible should add humus to the soil in the form of leafmould, peat, compost or green material such as grass mowings and old cabbage leaves.

The term "Immune" as applied to certain varieties means that they are immune only to wart disease and not to anything else and in districts where wart disease may be prevalent, only varieties described as "Immune" should be planted.

Varieties.
First Early: Arran Pilot, Duke of York, Epicure, Home Guard, Pentland Beauty and Sharpes Express.

Second Earlies: Craigs Royal, Dunbar Rover, Great Scot, Maris Peer.

Main crop: Arran Peak, Dr. McIntosh, Pentland Crown, King Edward VII and Majestic. The latter suits all soils but sometimes is rather an ugly shape.

Sweet Corn

This is still not a popular crop despite the fact that varieties are now available which will fruit in almost any district.

A light to medium soil suits it admirably and heavy, retentive soils in cold districts can be made suitable by raising it into bed-form as recommended for asparagus. That is, take out a pathway on each side of the bed some 3–4 feet wide and place the soil taken out of a path 6 inches deep and 2 feet wide on the bed. This not only makes the soil deeper, but drier and warmer. Any reasonable garden soil which would grow any other vegetable crop will grow sweet corn.

In few districts it is advisable to plant the seed directly in the ground mainly because waiting for the soil to warm up would shorten the growing period. Seeds can be successfully germinated in the soil under cloches or even under inverted jam jars, but in most areas especially for the home gardener, they should be raised in soil blocks or pots in a greenhouse or frame and planted out when danger of frost is passed.

90

Sweet corn is wind-pollinated, and so this is a crop best grown in a block rather than in one single row. Naturally, the home gardener will require only a comparatively few plants and to plant these in a single row across the garden may result in disappointment. Plant in a group with the plants about 8–12 inches apart each way.

Only experience will teach the exact time at which to gather, but an indication may be had from the heard or silk as this dries up when it has fulfilled its function of collecting pollen.

Varieties.
John Innes Hybrid (Canada Cross), Kelvedon Glory, Prima.

Tomato var. Sugar Plum

Tomatoes   It would take more than a whole book to do justice to the culture of the tomato, but once the principles of culture are understood it becomes the easiest of vegetables to grow. The descriptive term vegetable is used here as it is by common usage listed as a vegetable in seed catalogues and in show schedules.

This crop is more coddled and worried over than perhaps any other but to be understood it should be regarded rather as a temperamental Latin film star than our well acclimatized vegetable. But even in our variable climate with its cold dampness it does show a surprising adaptability and tolerance for the often unsatisfactory conditions under which it is grown. Weight for area of ground it can produce nearly ten times more weight of crop than the potato.

It is, however, essential to provide a warm, well-drained soil and plenty of air and light. The richness or otherwise of the soil is not a matter of great moment provided that it gives a free root-run as the tomato is such an accommodating plant that even starting from pure sand sufficient nutrients can be added for it to give a decent crop. Plants may be grown in the garden, in beds in the greenhouse heated or unheated, in boxes and pots and in frames or under cloches. The more extended the period of warmth, the longer will be the cropping season, thus in a cold greenhouse the crop could easily be one-third that of a heated greenhouse and the crop from an unheated greenhouse in the more northerly counties will be much less than in the warmer south.

Ordinary garden soil may be used provided some material such as fibrous sedge peat is added to prevent the finer particled soil of the garden from becoming compacted following repeated watering. Air is essential to the roots of plants, so if the soil settles down too hard then neither air nor water can get down to the roots.

A well-drained soil is a warmer soil than a wet soggy one and if no other method is employed for warming such as by pipes or soil heating cables, then raising it above the level of the surrounding garden will help matters considerably.

It is rarely wise to dig a hole in the greenhouse to make a special bed for tomatoes as in many cases this merely becomes a sump into which water will drain. Far better to make a retaining kerb to the bed or border and add more soil, this will not only ensure a deeper root run but the soil will be warmer and better drained.

Perhaps the easiest and most trouble-free way of growing tomatoes for home use is to grow them by the "Ring" method, which is a combination of the soil and nutrient method of cultivation.

Ring method of growing tomatoes

This method is an old one which has been revived during recent years and has a lot to recommend it. The main advantages are, an average increase of crop yield by about 3lbs. per plant, 75 per cent less soil is needed and no danger of the plants suffering from the roots drying out even if unable to water them for a week or more. Furthermore, the soil is much warmer than soil in a bed and a better root action results.

The most interesting point technically is that there are in effect, two root systems, one in the "ring" in soil and one in the material under the ring. This is how it works.

All gardeners know that if a plant in a pot is stood on soil or ashes then roots will eventually find their way out of the bottom of the pot into the moist material on which they are standing. And that if fertilisers are applied to the roots in the gravel or the bench, the plant will benefit considerably. This, then, is the principle of the ring method.

In practice, the tomato plants are planted in bottomless containers which may be of any material, but if this method is to be used annually then permanent containers such as concrete or drainage tiles are suggested. Although called "rings" these bottomless containers are most conveniently made square, about the size of a biscuit tin is most convenient.

To prepare for the change, take all the soil out of the beds to a depth of at least 12 inches and if the sub-soil is clay, arrange for it to drain either into a sump or lead it to a drain outside. Not so much because of the amount of water that will be used, but because of it being lower than the ground outside, water will seep in from the surrounding garden and may become a bed full of water. A fate, by the way, which happens to many tomato beds, sweet peas and celery trenches and accounts for a lot of losses.

Fill in the bed with ashes, gravel or coarse sand, taking care to put the clinkers or larger stones at the bottom with a layer of the sifted material on the top. Not too fine, a half-inch riddle is fine enough, and for the neat-minded folk this can be topped up with granite or limestone chippings or Dorset pebbles.

Stand the containers on the surface at twenty-inch centres, i.e. when the plants are put in, the stems will be 20 inches apart each way. Fill in the "rings" (containers) with a good lumpy soil. If you have turf, chop it up with a spade mixing in 2 parts of rotted manure to 7 parts soil with half a part of coarse sand if the soil is heavy.

93

Add lime rubble or crushed limestone at the rate of an 8-inch potful to a barrowload of the mixture. To each barrowload add a 6-inch potful of bonemeal and a 4-inch potful of sulphate of potash. Mix this all thoroughly and allow to stand for a week and mix again. This is a point so often missed by many amateurs. This mixing, rest, and mixing adds very materially to the manurial value of the mixing. Put this into the containers and press down very firmly without actually ramming it. During the operation of filling you will not fail to notice how much less soil is required, a real boon in these days when soil is so scarce.

One further advantage of this method is that the actual preparations for planting can be delayed until the last moment, provided the soil has been mixed beforehand. This means that the ash bed can be used for standing out boxes of seedlings and cuttings and can, in fact, be used for this purpose after the "rings" have been put in position and filled.

If the mixed soil in the heap is very cold, it can easily be warmed by heating two or three bricks and burying these in the heap for an hour or so. See that the soil is reasonably moist before filling the rings so that no water is required for a day or two after planting. This is a practice which should be followed, i.e. no water for a week or so after planting.

Watering a soil consolidates it and drives out the air. Better feeding roots form in a soil which contains cavities filled with water vapour. This is why you are always advised never to sift soil for pot plants and why I always stipulate a fibrous peat when a substitute for turf is required. Sufficient moisture will be provided for about a fortnight or three weeks if the ashes are watered over with a rosed can two or three times a week. It will also wash out any impurities left in the ashes.

When watering starts, water the "rings" without a rose, directing the water around the inside edges, gradually working to the centre without actually wetting the leaves and stem of the plant. Later on when the temperature is higher and the plant stronger, this will not matter so much.

Keep the soil in the ring moist at all times. Fortunately it is impossible to over-water, but excess water will tend to wash the fertiliser out of the soil too quickly and down into the ashes faster than the roots can follow it.

With every watering, weak solutions of plant food are being washed down into the ashes and the roots will follow fast until it becomes necessary to give more feed, this time on the ashes. When the first and second trusses have been formed and the third truss is just setting, is the best time for this. Give each plant a heaped dessert-spoonful of dried blood or a teaspoonful of sulphate of ammonia and gently wash this into the soil with about a half a gallon of water, applied to the ring. After this, all the actual feeding should be done on the bed of ashes and not into the rings.

The golden rule is never to use any great amounts of fertiliser at one time and always in soluble form. Do not dust the fertiliser on the ashes in a dry powder form unless it is immediately soluble and capable of being washed in straight away. Ordinary commercial chemicals are fast being superseded by these more soluble types for intensive and greenhouse culture. Although at first sight they may appear dear, they work out more cheaply because of the waste in the others which tend to cake and quickly become insoluble in the soil and the plants can only take up a very small proportion.

It is only necessary to give a feed once a month to the roots in the "rings"; plain water will keep the soil moist. Apply the soluble fertiliser to the bed with a coarse rosed can, a teaspoonful to two gallons of water is sufficient and this will treat 2 sq. yds. About once a month during the height of summer, give twice this amount of clear water to the bed.

If you object to chemicals you can use ordinary liquid manure, but as this does not contain the essential elements in the same concentration, the same heavy crops cannot be expected.

A variation of the method can be used with great advantage when a few plants are grown at the base of a warm wall or fence. Instead of a more elaborate preparation of a bed near the foundations of the house, the soil is merely dug over and the bottomless containers filled with soil are placed close to the wall and treated in exactly the same way as described for greenhouse culture, thus effecting an enormous saving in time and materials.

Grown purely outdoors as a vegetable crop without protection of cloches or a wall, is something of a gamble except in favoured districts, but by using the dwarf varieties, such as Amateur and Puck, reasonable crops may be had.

The soil for outdoor tomatoes must not be too well manured otherwise the fruits will be too big and coarse, this is due to the fact that there is little control over the moisture they may receive. So it is better to start with unmanured soil and rely on feeding and mulches to improve the fertility. When selecting a position it should be in the open, away from overhanging trees and the shade of buildings and not be on the site previously occupied by potatoes.

Well hardened plants may be planted outdoors in early June at 18 inches between the plants and if more than one row is planted, 2 feet 6 inches between the rows. Stake each plant at the time of planting and tie up the plant at intervals during the growing season. If a wire is stretched between two strong posts, the top of the stakes can be tied to it.

Single Stem Method.
Cultural work during the growing season consists of removing the side shoots which appear in the axils of the tall upright growing varieties. Rub them out when about 2 inches long. On no account leave them until they get very big and have to be cut out with a knife as this only takes the strength away from the plant.

Pinch the top out, when four trusses have been made, one or two leaves above the last truss.

Multi-Stem Method.
This method produces the heaviest crops of all and as much as 30lbs. per plant can be gathered from plants trained in this way. For these it is necessary to put up strong wires between posts with the wires 6–8 inches apart in the same way as wires are arranged for fruit trees. The plants are planted 4 feet apart and when they are a foot high the tops are pinched out and four or five side growths are trained fan-wise on the wire. These in turn are stopped after four trusses have been made on each. Trained in this way, as many as 16–20 trusses on one plant are possible but, of course, to produce this weight of fruit extra food must be given. Tall varieties can be used for training in this way and excellent results have also been obtained with the variety Stonors Dwarf Gem.

The reader must be warned, however, that this method is only practicable below a rough line drawn across the country starting at the Yorkshire–Lincolnshire boundary.

Feeding should be adjusted according to the growth made, which in turn depends on the fertility of the soil, and season. A rough guide, however, is that if the stems are thick and the leaves lush, the plants will not require any nitrogenous fertilisers such as dried blood or sulphate of ammonia. Watering with 1oz. of sulphate of potash once or twice during the season will, however, tend to check exhuberant growth and improve the quality of the fruit. Watering with super-phosphate at the same rate when the fruit is of usable size will accelerate ripening.

For normal purposes, weak liquid manure made by suspending

animal droppings in a tub of water, given at fortnightly intervals, or alternatively about four applications of a good proprietary tomato fertiliser during the season will produce a good crop.

Raising Plants.
Nothing has been said so far about raising plants which is normally done by sowing seeds in a heated greenhouse from December onwards for earliest crops under glass, up to August when plants are raised in a cold frame for winter fruiting.

For many people this is not a worthwhile proposition as it entails the maintaining of a temperature of 50°–55°F. (10°–13°C.) for a long period. Plants raised under cooler conditions from seed sown in April will be suitable for outside culture, as the hardier they are raised the less will be the shock and check to growth when they are planted in the open garden.

Where plants are bought from a nurseryman it is strongly advised that an order be placed several months ahead. Do this in writing and state clearly for what purpose they are required, warm greenhouse, unheated greenhouse, or outdoors, giving the date on which they are required. This will greatly assist the nurseryman and will enable him to arrange his programme with the greatest benefit to the customer. Avoid if possible, the casual last minute purchase of plants from a shop or market stall for if tomato plants are chilled they will take weeks to recover even under the best of conditions. If you do fetch your own plants from the nursery, see that each plant is rolled in a sheet of newspaper to protect it from cold winds. As was said at the beginning of the chapter, the tomato is easy to grow but it will not tolerate sudden changes of temperature, and exposure to a low temperature and especially cold winds, will set them back two or three weeks.

Varieties.
Ailsa Craig, an old but excellent variety remarkable for its good flavour; Best of All, smooth fruit of good form with few seeds; Big Boy, a very large variety, the fruits often weighing more than one pound and therefore suitable for slicing; Harbinger, a heavy cropping early tomato for greenhouse and outdoor use; Moneymaker, medium sized fruits of good quality; Outdoor Girl, an early variety most suitable for growing outdoors.

A number of F.1 hybrid tomatoes are now in cultivation including: Eurocross, Growers Pride, Sioux and Supercross. Yellow fruited variety—Golden Perfection.

Dwarf Tomatoes These are a comparatively new introduction and are well worthy of consideration by the home grower, as even with very little skilled attention fair crops of good quality fruit can be had.

They will grow on any good garden soil but, like the taller types, a site formerly occupied by potatoes should be avoided. The addition of 2ozs. of bonemeal and 1½ozs. of sulphate of potash per sq. yd. to soil as prepared for any other crop mentioned in this book is all that is required. Firm the soil well after planting, by treading, and revive the flattened surface by stirring with a dutch hoe, as this firmness helps to control exhuberant growth and lessens the tendency to produce coarse fruits.

This is an admirable cloche crop and the area prepared for their reception should be covered at least a week before planting so that it warms up nicely. If the plants are to remain under cloches until the crop has been gathered the large barn should be used, as although the dwarf variety Amateur only grows about a foot in height when grown outdoors, it is inevitable that under the more favourable conditions under glass, at least another 6–9 inches of height will be added.

As some fruit from these dwarf tomatoes must trail on the ground the soil under the plant should be covered with a generous mulch of non-dusty fibrous peat tailings. This will not only prevent slug damage, but will discourage weeds and keep the soil moist as well. Do not make the mistake of lifting the cloches to water under them, as this encourages fungus diseases. It is quite sufficient to apply all the water required along the outside edges of the cloches; in fact, during dry weather if a hose pipe is directed so that the water falls on the cloches sufficient moisture will run down the glass and find its way to the roots.

Reliable bush varieties are: Easicrop, Histon Cropper and The Amateur.

In the early part of the season greenfly may attack the young growths, but a dusting with an insecticidal powder such as nicotine dust or derris will take care of these. A dust under cloches is to be preferred to spraying.

Pests and Diseases.
The diseases of tomatoes like those of the potato are many and quite a number attack the plants for the simple reason that they belong to the same family group. At the same time many are preventable diseases and a strict attention to cleanliness and hygiene in garden and greenhouse will materially reduce the risk.

Cleanliness in a garden does not mean a well-cut lawn or a well-kept path or border, but the prompt removal of all diseased and decaying debris and the efficient disposal or deep burying of diseased fruits, mildewed leaves and the like, as eggs of pests and spores of diseases are carried over from one season to another and from one crop to another. Thus, what may have started off as a mild attack may develop into an epidemic and what is more, soil and buildings and fittings may become so infested and infected that the growing of certain crops may have to be discontinued.

In the greenhouse adequate ventilation is essential—advice easily given and written but often difficult for the amateur gardener to translate into the everyday acts of opening and closing doors and ventilators, and quite frankly, can only be acquired by the perception of a plant's comfort and response. As all greenhouse plants are in the first instance outdoor plants an appreciation of this will help, remembering that they want fresh air without cold draughts.

Outdoor tomatoes have far fewer troubles than those grown in greenhouses due to the fact that the plants are hardier and get an abundance of fresh air. For the full treatment of tomatoes under glass the reader must seek this in books written specifically on this subject.

The most serious troubles likely to attack outdoor tomatoes are fungus diseases but if the plants are sprayed with a good fungicide such as Bordeaux mixture at the stage when the fruits on the lower trusses are about the size of marbles it will give them a protective film. Do not be alarmed at the bluish coating which appears on the leaves at first, this is harmless and is the protective film referred to.

In some diseases, birds pecking the ripening fruit may be the most serious pest and to avoid damage, gather the fruits when they begin to change colour and place in a dark drawer. Exposure to sunlight is not necessary for the ripening of tomatoes, actually they do this more readily in total darkness.

Turnips

This vegetable is a very valuable one as it is one of the few that can be had in use in good condition the year through. Its food value is high and the vitamin content of the green tops is the highest of any vegetable grown, but for some reason turnips are not as widely used as they should be. Stored swede turnips, for example, have the merit that they can be mixed with parsnips or carrots and provide a welcome change from the monotony of a single vegetable.

White Turnips These mature, or rather, are at their best when grown in about 6–8 weeks. When allowed to remain much longer they become hot and stringy, whereas a crisp, succulent, white turnip is a most attractive vegetable especially when roasted in its jacket.

It is not worthwhile transplanting seedlings so that are sown where they are to grow in drills, or the seed scattered thinly on the surface of a piece of ground which has previously been dug and manured and then raked in. Wherever possible plenty of organic matter such as compost, leafmould, peat, etc., should be dug in to hold moisture during a dry period and it is not always practicable to water.

As they do not mind a little shade they are a useful crop to sow near trees or buildings or between taller crops. The more thinly the seed is sown the less will be the work of thinning, which is necessary when the plants are about 2 inches high, to 3 inches apart. If grown by the wide drill method they can be used freely as soon as about the size of a table-tennis ball. A great mistake is invariably made in sowing too thickly: this should be avoided as the seed germinates freely. The earliest crops may be sown in February, but for general use in the garden, seed may be sown at intervals until the end of July. Only small quantities should be sown at any one time so that they can always be had in the peak of condition, it being a simple matter to scatter a few seeds on a small patch of ground and rake them in without going to the bother of putting down a line. If only one boiling is raised from a small sowing it is better than having a fine row of roots as big as footballs which are completely uneatable.

Two good varieties of early white turnip are Early Snowball and White Milan.

The late sown batch may be left in the ground over winter and when the young growth starts in spring they will provide a supply of tasty, health-giving greens.

It is not necessary to try to store white turnips as their charm is in youth and succulence and are best supplemented by a sowing of an orange or yellow fleshed variety which is slower growing and in consequence lasts longer in good eating condition. Swede turnips are excellent eating and can be stored almost until the first of the white turnips are ready. The seed is sown in May, for this main storing crop, in an open situation and thinned out to about 10–12 inches apart and 18 inches between the rows.

If the soil is in reasonably good condition no feeding will be necessary and the firmer will be the flesh. In late autumn they may be lifted and stored in a cool shed or cellar, or they may be covered with soil where they are growing—frost will not harm them. Blanched shoots of swedes are a fine dish, and, like spinach beet may be boiled and pickled and are excellent with cold beef.

As these belong to the brassica (cabbage) family, growing them on ground following this crop should be avoided as they are liable to club root disease.

Like cabbage, they need a dressing of lime and a soil in good heart which will reduce the risk of this disease.

There are garden varieties of swedes, but these never seem to have the same flavour as the field variety Purple Top. Give these the most exposed position in the garden for nothing is hardier.

The main pest is the flea beetle or turnip fly which attacks the leaves, riddling them with small holes. As a preventative and control, dust the leaves and along the rows with gamma or derris powder or any other dust currently recommended.

Club root disease, which is a fungus and a serious menace to all cruciferous crops, is in my opinion, widely distributed in farmyard manure. Please refer to club root under brassica crops.

Vegetable marrow var. Table Dainty

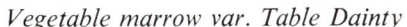

Vegetable Marrows The cultivation of marrows is similar to that of cucumbers, but as they produce fewer fruits and the seeds and plants are cheaper, more plants can be grown without any special soil preparation. In normal garden soil it is sufficient to take out a couple of spadesful of soil and put in a forkful of rotted manure covering this with soil and planting on top.

Marrows are not highly favoured as a vegetable but have the merit of being a digestive and assist in the comfortable assimilation of meats like pork. Baby marrows are a great delicacy and are widely used at the best restaurants when about 5—6 inches long and about 2 inches in diameter. Cut down the centre to form two halves, scoop out the immature seeds and fill with shrimps, do not peel but use each boat-shaped half as a container and cook in hot fat preferably butter.

Except in the most favoured districts young plants planted out in late May or early June should receive the same protection as advised for cucumbers so that they get away to a good start without a check to growth.

There are several types and varieties of marrow and for the small garden perhaps the most convenient and useful type are the bush varieties which do not produce long trailing stems and form small upright plants covering an area of only a few square feet. With the bush varieties no stopping or pinching out is necessary, and little stopping is required for trailing marrows, the usual practice being to pinch out the top when about a foot high and thereafter allow the plant to wander about at will.

Where the marrow differs radically from the cucumber is that the flowers of the marrow must be fertilised before the fruits will swell. Where only one plant is grown it may be difficult to have both male and female flowers open at the same time. Another point in favour of the bush marrow is that several may be grown in the space occupied by one trailing marrow. In favourable seasons insects and bees can be relied upon to transfer the pollen from the male flower to the female. Like the cucumber the female flower is easily identified even in the bud stage by the miniature or embryo marrow behind the yellow flower.

If the flowers are examined carefully it will be seen that inside the female flowers there are three knob-like stamens but inside the male only one. As the male flower is of no value after it has produced the pollen which is ready almost as soon as the flower opens, the flower can be plucked and the petals carefully bent back or torn off. The pollen-covered pistil should then be gently stroked across the stamens inside the female flower so that as much of the pollen as possible is transferred. Choose a dry period for this, as due to the fact that marrow flowers are usually carried erect to invite the attentions of insects, the pollen often gets wet.

Marrows may be used at any stage and for a vegetable they are perhaps at their best when about 12–18 inches long, but they can, however, be allowed to ripen on the plant and stored for several months.

When they are to be used for storing or for show purposes it is essential that they be laid on a sheet of glass or slate as the slightest pressure—even their own weight on the soil will mark their delicate skin.

Gather when ripe—found by gently tapping with the knuckles, when they will sound hollow. Sever from the plant and place in a net and hang in a cool frost-proof place where they can be kept till April.

Exhibitors might like to know that judges test the age and tenderness of an exhibit by tapping and by gently pressing a thumbnail into the flower end.

Varieties.
Bush green, bush white, zucchini, an early variety of bushy habit with emerald-green fruit. Early Gem is an F.1 hybrid. Courgette is really a bush marrow of which the fruit is cut when 6 or 8 in. long. These are cooked in their entirety and are delicious when boiled and served with oiled butter or white sauce. The so called Vegetable Spaghetti can be grown in the same way as vegetable marrows. When ripe, the whole fruit is boiled for 20 to 30 minutes. It is then cut in half and seeds and flesh removed. After seasoning with salt, pepper, butter and sauce the fruit is served cold with salads.

Ridge cucumbers

4   Salads

There is no hard and fast definition of what constitutes the ingredients of a salad as these may range from cooked vegetables like peas and potatoes to raw cauliflower and carrots and from the leaves of the nasturtium to the flowers of the calendula and anchusa. This extension of salad-making materials is all to the good and as an encouragement to further extension of fruit, flowers and vegetables for this purpose, it can be stated that any tender succulent growths of all herbs and vegetables may be used.

The whole accent must be, however, on "tender and succulent"; as an example, the crisp tender hearts of a cabbage or savoy are often a far superior ingredient of a salad than a flabby lettuce with leaves looking and tasting like wet blotting paper.

It is not essential that the subjects used should be fully grown and mature. For example, small beetroot about the size of a golf ball are ideal, and lettuce seedlings with only a few leaves can be used. These may be grown specially in pots or boxes and cut off level with the soil in the same way as cress, and a continuous supply of this may be had through the year under the most primitive of glass structures.

Lettuce, mustard and cress, however, will generally form the backbone of any salad and a variety of lettuce called Salad Bowl which is a large, spreading type, from which leaves may be pulled as required.

The cress usually bought in punnets in the shops is rather a mystery to many people. Called cress—looks like mustard, is in fact neither, but is rape and a coarse member of the cabbage family. When fully grown it has no merit as a vegetable and is only fit for cattle or for digging into the soil as green manure. When in the seedling leaf stage, however, it is an excellent salading material being milder in flavour than the larger seeded, much hotter tasting mustard, besides the seed which is produced in large quantities is much cheaper. Curiously enough, although so widely grown commercially as a salad the seed is seldom offered in catalogues in small quantities, but any seedsman will supply small quantities on request.

Seeds of rape, mustard and cress, are sown on the surface of prepared soil in boxes or where large quantities are required on the finely-raked surface of special beds. The boxes are first soaked and the seed sown evenly and thinly on the surface and is not covered with soil but pressed down into it with a flat board. The reason being that seedlings will be less gritty than if the seed was covered in the ordinary way. If the box is covered with a sheet of glass and then covered with paper the growth will be greatly accelerated and the stems will be longer.

Any seeds of the brassica family such as cabbage, sprouts, cauliflower, etc., which are surplus to ordinary requirements can be treated in this way and the taste will be indistinguishable from commercial cress. A greenhouse is not essential to grow this, any window in the house or shed will provide sufficient light.

An onion flavouring is often desirable in a salad and this may be had in a variety of ways. Onions and shallots which have been stored over winter will often start into growth and if the bulbs have become soft and useless for cooking, allow the tops to grow in a dim light and they will produce pale green mild-flavoured, crisp growths. More conventional sources of onion flavouring are chives, immature shallots, seedling onions (scallions), Welsh onions and tree onions. Chives are miniature leek-like growths which grow in clusters and for use a small bunch is cut at ground level to be chopped finely for mixing in the salad bowl. These can be grown from seed or by clumps purchased from most seed firms and will grow in any soil and under practically any conditions. They make a useful and decorative edging to a path especially when in flower, their bluish purple-headed flowers looking most attractive.

The Welsh onion is a much larger version of the chives with a similar habit of growth, but being much larger, a portion of the clump can be detached and as the individual growths are as big as an ordinary spring onion they may be peeled and used whole in the salad.

Propagation is by seed in the first instance and as they are perpetual, large clumps can be divided into smaller portions and replanted in April.

It is useful to have clumps of herbs and salad material handy to the kitchen door so it is convenient to pop out as fancy dictates.

Capsicum

Frequently seen in shops this subject is not cultivated as much as it deserves. The plants can be raised in the same way as aubergines. Sow the seed in a temperature of 60 deg.F. in February or March and eventually pot on the plants so that they are finally in the 6 or 7 in. size. They can be grown in the cool greenhouse or once hardened can be placed under frames or cloches.

The plants grow 2 to $2\frac{1}{2}$ ft. tall, the white flowers being followed by fruit, which colours according to variety. Capsicums vary in length from 4 to 5 in. although with the bull-nosed types the fruit is thicker and shorter.

Chinese Cabbage

Pe-Tsai, Wong Bok, Michikli are forms of cabbage which although they may be cooked are best used as salading. Although hardy they are better sown under cloches so that they grow quickly and tenderly, and in northern districts may require covering in autumn. Culture as for ordinary cabbage in normal garden soil.

Cucumber

Like the leek, the cucumber has been used as an article of diet from earliest times and is a valuable adjunct to the salad and enjoys the distinction that of all vegetables only a cucumber can taste like a cucumber and the nearest smell to it are the leaves of nemesia.

In this book, only the treatment of outdoor types will be dealt with as the detailed cultivation of these more exotic types would require much more space than is available.

Cucumbers, like marrows and melons, are tender plants; cold will check their growth and the slightest touch of frost will kill them, so all growth must take place between the late frosts of May and the early ones of September.

Unless a greenhouse is available for raising the plants from seed in early April, it is best to buy plants in pots or soil blocks in early June. Even then they get away to a better start if they can be given the protection of cloche or frame.

The best crops are grown on a purely organic compost such as a manure or rubbish heap or failing this luxury, a barrow-load of decayed vegetable matter such as rotted straw, spent mushroom beds, leaves or garden-made compost.

One or at the most two plants will suffice, as several dozen fruits can be had from one plant. Choose a site sheltered from cold winds and near a water supply as they are thirsty plants. Make a hole in the ground about 9 inches deep and break up the bottom and into this tip a good barrow-load of the material described. Arrange this in a conical heap and cover it with the soil excavated from the hole to which has been added a 3-inch potful of bonemeal. Firm gently but do not tread hard, as the object is to leave a mound about 12–15 inches high filled with an organic mixture. Prepare the mound about a fortnight in advance of planting and cover with a cloche with the ends closed with glass. If no cloches are available, make use of a bottomless box covered with glass. This device will be found most useful for protecting marrows, cucumbers and melons for several weeks after planting. The larger it is the longer it can remain over the plant, but it should not be more than 12 inches deep.

Train the plant by pinching out the growing point (tip of plant) after it has been planted about a fortnight, this will have the advantage of making it produce lateral growths from above the leaves. In a frame these side growths may be allowed to reach the sides of the frame before the tips of these in turn are pinched again. Outdoors, without frame protection, stop them when they have made about 2ft. of growth.

A cucumber produces both female and male flowers which differ only in that it is the female flower which produces the cucumber. Even in the bud stage the embryo cucumber is clearly visible behind   107 the flower. Male flowers are merely yellow and cone-shaped on a thin stalk and are best removed not only to concentrate the energy of the plant into the production of cucumbers, but because if the female flowers become fertilised by insects then the seeds will swell and the fruit will become bitter and uneatable.

Readers will do well to familiarize themselves with the appearance of a male and female flower, for in the case of marrows, fertilisation is essential; a practice directly opposed to cucumber cultivation. All along the lateral growths, embryo cucumbers should appear at every leaf joint and from near the same point, sub-laterals will appear. Allow these to develop until a young cucumber appears on these sub-laterals and then pinch out the tip, one leaf beyond the embryo cucumber. When they start producing and the first young fruits are an inch or so long, the plant will need some additional food, mainly nitrogenous, such as manure and soot water or the more easily applied dried blood. Dust a heaped dessertspoonful on the heap and water it in, feed at least once a fortnight and never allow the roots of the plant to become dry. Always use aired water as water straight from an underground tank can be colder than tap water in summer.

Good varieties include: Bedfordshire Prize Ridge, Burpee Hybrid, Stockwood Ridge and the newer Burpless Early an F.1 hybrid. This has dark green fruits 10 to 12in. long and as with other varieties of Japanese introduction it is not bitter or indigestible.

The small fruited outdoor gherkins are much used for pickling.

Apple Cucumber, sometimes known as Lemon Cucumber and Crystal Apple, is a roundish variety, pale greenish-yellow in colour and is easier to digest than the ordinary types. Very prolific and can be trained up a trellis like a gourd. One plant of mine produced 80 fruits.

It has the additional merit that one fruit is sufficient for four persons and portions of cut cucumbers need not be stood about in jars until they are required again. If cucumbers upset your digestion slice thinly but do not peel them.

Treat plants in frames in the same manner, do not ventilate but shade the glass with whitewash and to prevent loss of moisture mulch the surface of the frame with rotted manure which should be sprayed night and morning.

Dandelions and Lambs Lettuce

Lambs lettuce or corn salad is very much like a large cultivated dandelion and is useful as a salad ingredient in that it can be had all the year round if a first sowing is made in April and a second one in July and covered with cloches as growth slows up in September.

Seeds are sown in shallow drills and the plants thinned out to about 6 inches apart in the rows, with 15 inches between the rows. Only young crisp leaves should be used and if they are found too bitter for personal taste then a box or plant pots placed over a few plants for a day or two will partially blanch them and reduce the bitterness.

Garlic

This requires warm, dry conditions and is not suited to every district, growing better in the warmer southern counties. Reproduction is by planting clove-like portions about 2 inches under the soil about six inches apart..

Few people will really want to grow this as dried cloves can be obtained at any delicatessen store and will keep for a long time. Some gardeners, however, will like to grow their own if only for the interest of doing it.

Potato Onion

This is rarely seen nowadays, but in districts where other types are difficult to grow this is a most useful onion as it appears to be immune from pests and diseases. The flavour is strong and in appearance looks like a cross between a shallot and a red Spanish onion. It gets its name from the fact that it is planted about 5 inches deep in the soil and for each bulb planted it produces four to five others in a cluster like a shallot. As it grows, it gradually works its way to the top of the soil, until in August the shoulders of the bulbs are near the surface. From these the soil should be carefully scraped with the finger to assist ripening.

Tree Onions

Although useful and interesting these are not worth while growing as a crop from which a heavy yield could be expected. The habit of this plant is unusual in that the small clusters of purplish-coloured bulbs are borne on the tips of the onion-like leaves.

They are grown from seed in the first instance and propagated thereafter by pressing single bulbs into ordinary garden soil. As the stems become top-heavy as the clusters swell, it is necessary to stake the plants to prevent them being damaged by wind.

Use as any other onion.

Pumpkins and Squashes

Like the marrow, pumpkins and squashes are not widely grown, but since the influx of American troops, pumpkin pie is at least known if not appreciated.

If not widely grown the choice of variety is extremely wide in size colour and flavour, ranging from small types about the size of a cricket ball to monsters weighing a half hundredweight or more.

The cultivation is exactly the same as the marrow except in the case where very large fruit is required, then they should be limited to one or at the most, two per plant.

Nothing is lost in quality no matter how large they grow and as they are in great demand for harvest festival or for competitions a few remarks how to produce giant specimens may not come amiss.

As the bulk is largely water it goes without saying that they must be watered and fed almost daily as soon as the fruit is set. Allow several fruits to set and very soon it will be seen which one is going to be the biggest. Cut off the unwanted fruits and pinch out the growing point of all laterals and stop each sub-lateral, removing all flowers, male and female as they appear.

Accompany each watering with at least two gallons of weak liquid manure either made from sheep or poultry droppings or dried blood and soot water. Mulch, too, with a barrow-load of partially rotted manure. When nearly ripe, sink a 2lb. jam jar in the ground close to the stem of the fruit, then take a darning needle and thread with thick rug or berlin wool. Pass the needle through the stem of the fruit and pull a double thickness of wool through leaving the ends long enough to reach the bottom of the jar to form a wick. Fill this with a solution of sugar and water using a dessertspoonful to a 2lb. jar. The fruit will absorb quite a lot of this and plump up a bit more. Fruits of 80lbs. can be obtained in this way.

Varieties.
Large—King of the Mammoths.
Cheese pumpkin, flattened, ribbed fruits.
Acorn Squash. Small, can be baked in its skin.
Turks Cap. Small, very decorative.
Rotherside Orange. Small and round, lovely flavour.
Noodle Squash. When cooked in skin, flesh falls out like noodles. When cooked in skins make a small hole in one end or they may burst.

Radish

This crop does not need a deep soil and can be grown on heavy clay as well as sand so long as the site has been properly prepared. The chief aim should be to provide a fine soil for lumpy ground will never produce good succulent roots. It is also essential that the soil never dries out.

This is another salad crop and seed should be sown little and often so that fresh crisp roots are available over a long period. Varieties include: Cherry Bell, a scarlet globe shaped variety with crisp white flesh; French Breakfast, most popular with scarlet and white tipped roots; Icicle is a long white. China Rose Winter has long blunt ended roots and sown in summer it is hardy and most valuable for winter use.

An early crop can be secured by sowing under frames, while the French Breakfast Forcing type can be sown in a temperature of 55 deg.F. resulting in roots being ready for picking about three weeks, after sowing.

Herbs including Balm, Fennel, Rue, Morjoram, Sage, Thyme and Rosemary

5   Herbs

There is a wide range of these but housewives appear to have forgotten how to use them or cannot be bothered to dry and preserve them nowadays.

Seeds of the following are readily available and although a few can only be grown satisfactorily in the southern counties, most of them can be grown in any district.

Angelica, Anise, Balm, Basil, Borage, Caraway, Chervil, Coriander, Dill, Fennel, Finocchio, Hyssop, Horehound, Lovage, Marjoram, Marjoram Sweet, Mint, Pennyroyal, Purslame, Rampion, Rosemary, Rue, Sage, Savoury summer, Savoury winter, Sorrel, Southernwood, Sweet Basil, Sweet Cicely, Tarragon, Tansy, Thyme, Wormwood.

Although not comprehensive this is a formidable list and not everyone will want to grow all these unless it is intended to make a complete herb garden. As all of these have strongly scented leaves they are recommended for inclusion in gardens planted for sightless people.

It should be accepted as a general rule that the soil for practically all herbs should be of an open texture, well drained and sited in the warmest corner of the garden. And if the herb garden can be walled or angled in the corner formed by two walls the fragrance of the herbs released by the sun will be trapped.

In districts where the normal soil is thin and heavy, it is suggested that specially raised beds be used and as a number of these are of a perennial nature, permanent edgings to beds may be used. Work in plenty of peat to give bulk.

On a small scale a nice idea is to arrange three or four large stones in the form of a diamond or a triangle and fill the space enclosed with a light gritty soil. The advantage of this is that they are both decorative and useful, easy to maintain, especially by elderly persons, and deep-rooted plants can send their roots down into the soil underneath. At the same time the upper soil enclosed by the stones is warmer and drier and there is little risk of the plants drying out in winter time.

A suggested arrangement is for a bush of lavender or sage to be planted in the centre of an enclosure and for plants of thyme to be planted around the edge and allowed to trail down the stones forming the raised bed. An existing herbaceous border may be used and if ornamented rough limestone rocks are used it will enhance the beauty and usefulness of the garden. In country districts a raised border such as this along the southern front of a cottage is really something, especially if thyme is interspersed with sweet-smelling flowers such as pinks.

All these plants can be easily and readily raised from seed which is best done by sowing in pots or boxes of light soil stood in a cold frame or a box covered with a sheet of glass. Prick out the seedlings in boxes 2 inches apart and when large enough can be planted out in their permanent quarters.

Their uses are many and leaves and flowers may be used green in drinks or salads or dried when at the peak of their oil and aroma content, usually about August, in any case before they set their seeds as by that time a great deal of their fragrance has gone. Generally speaking, herbs that are used green will need a little rotted manure added to the soil, but those grown for drying will need practically none. Collect by cutting off sprigs of the herbs, tie in small bunches and hang in an airy place to dry, or if bottled, spread on paper in a cooling oven.

6 Vegetables in Greenhouses, Frames and Cloches

Fewer varieties of vegetable can be grown in greenhouses than can the varieties of flowers, mainly because their structure is different and cannot be conveniently placed in pots and other containers. It is, however, possible to advance or force asparagus, cauliflowers and peas although the results hardly justify the trouble, but French and Runner beans, lettuce, salads, mint and of course, tomatoes are not only worthwhile crops but very important commercially.

French beans will not only tolerate and thrive in high temperatures but will crop exceedingly well in unheated greenhouses, frames and are a very profitable crop. Naturally, where some form of heat is available an earlier start can be made, and in a small greenhouse growing them in large pots of about 9–10 inches diameter is undoubtedly the best way. A start can be made as early as January by placing some crocks or other form of drainage in the bottom and filling the pots two-thirds full of soil, gently firmed down. Stand these in the greenhouse for a few days to allow the soil to warm up and then sow five seeds in each pot by placing them on the top of the soil in the pot, covering them with about 2 inches of soil. They are not too particular as to soil, but if a good turfy loam, to which has been added 2 parts of rotted manure or coarse fibrous peat to 7 parts of soil with 2ozs. of superphosphate to each bushel of soil can be used, so much the better. (An ordinary bucket holds two gallons and four of these make a bushel.)

If, however, you want to make your own bushel measure, construct a rectangular box 22 inches long, 10 inches wide and 10 inches deep which will hold one bushel of compost.

The pots can be placed under the benches until the seeds germinate, then they must be stood near the glass to get as much light as possible. As the plants grow, support them with small twigs or canes and syringe daily with clear water. When they commence to bloom give an occasional feed with clear liquid manure or a soluble plant food. Alternatively, the seeds may be raised in boxes and planted in the soil of the greenhouse as for tomatoes, but for this method of cultivation it is recommended that the climbing French bean should be used. This is probably the heaviest cropper of all inside-grown beans and as they can be trained up strings and require approxi-

Cloche grown lettuce

mately the same conditions as tomatoes, they can be grown in the same greenhouse and alongside this crop.

A delicate variety for pot culture is the Golden Waxpod bean and for ordinary work use Masterpiece, a good early all-round variety. A suitable climbing variety is The Prince.

Runner beans are a wonderfully prolific crop for an unheated greenhouse where they can be treated in the same way as an outdoor crop and allowed to climb up canes, poles or string. If the pod clusters are judiciously thinned, huge tender beans, some 2ft. long, can be had from the variety Prizetaker.

Beans under glass must always have their blooms well sprayed as they will not set fruit if the air is at all dry, a condition which sometimes arises outdoors in hot weather and when they are grown up a sunny wall.

Although lettuces are extremely hardy and come through the most severe weather unharmed, naturally they cannot be expected to grow and mature outdoors between the months of October and

Lettuces

Broad beans flowering under cloches

April and as many greenhouses both heated and unheated are empty during this period, it is a worthwhile and profitable crop to grow.

Seeds can be sown thinly in boxes in September and as soon as the plants are large enough to handle should be pricked off into other boxes at 2 inches apart. These can be raised outdoors at this time of year or given the protection of a cold frame until the greenhouse is clear of a previous tomato crop. Merely dig over the cold soil, tread firmly and dust the soil with hydrated lime before raking and planting out at about 10 inches apart each way.

It is most important that any water given should not be splashed on the leaves and in damp districts it is recommended that the soil be ridged and the young plants planted on the tops of the ridges and the water applied to the hollows between the ridges. The maximum amount of fresh air should be given and doors and windows opened on all but foggy and drizzly days. It is not cold that harms them but a close stagnant atmosphere, which encourages botrytis and rot.

The selection of varieties for growing under glass is of the utmost importance and spare seed of summer varieties should not be used. The best varieties for this purpose are Cheshunt Early Giant, Cheshunt 5B and Kloek and Seaqueen, varieties which have been specially developed for quick maturing under glass during the short days of winter. For only small quantities lettuces may be planted singly in 6-inch pots and grown on as one would any other plant.

Mint

This may be forced in gentle heat and is grown on a large scale commercially, but for the small home grower a few sprigs of fresh mint in early spring is well worth the small amount of trouble involved.

Dig up a score or so root thongs from the outer edges of the rust free mint bed and it is from here the best roots will be found. Half fill a box about 4 inches deep with a light mixture of sand, peat or leafmould and soil in equal parts and lay the roots of the mint on this. Cover with soil to fill the box and water it thoroughly and stand on a bench in a warm greenhouse.

New Potatoes

Are excellent with fresh mint and may be grown successfully in large pots as recommended for French beans. No great amount of heat is required as the top growth would be too rapid and there would be few tubers underneath. A start can be made in January and a temperature of around 40°F. is quite high enough to start with.

Half fill a large plant pot, box or old bucket with soil and place on this one or even two potatoes, cover with an inch or two of soil. Later on as the plants grow, more soil can be gradually added to simulate the earthing process of outdoor potatoes, and as the top will be soft when grown under glass they must be supported with twigs or canes.

Any early variety may be used for this purpose but the variety Ulster Chieftain is especially recommended as this has a short haulm. There is a novel way of producing a boiling or two of new potatoes during the winter months which can actually be had for Christmas dinner without a greenhouse or heat of any kind.

To do this select a number of seed potatoes at planting time and thread these on a piece of wire about a yard long, bending one end to form a stop and the other to form a hook. Hang these up in an open shed or outdoors out of the direct rays of the sun and leave them like this until the end of August. Then prepare a box 7–8 inches deep and put in a layer of dry peat or straw. Place the potatoes singly on this bottom layer 3–4 inches apart and cover with a 4-inch layer of peat or with enough straw packed over them to prevent the light getting to them.

Leave them exactly like this in a dry, cool place until Christmas when it will be found that each odd tuber has produced a cluster of from six to eight new ones. Handle carefully and pull off only those big enough to use and put the others back and cover them again. Repeat until all are used up. The writer has done this every Christmas for over thirty years with never a failure.

Frame Culture

Any crop which can be grown in a greenhouse with the exception of climbing beans can be grown in a garden frame. But in the frame to those already mentioned, cauliflowers may be added as the conditions in a cold frame are much cooler than the greenhouse. Sow the seeds of a variety, such as All the Year Round in August, and pot up the resultant plants into 3-inch pots, and as they grow pot on into 5-inch pots and finally into 7-inch pots. Keep these outdoors until frost threatens and then place in the frame, give plenty of air and the crop will mature in early spring.

119

Cloches   These small structures of glass and wire are invaluable in helping the gardener to extend his growing season no matter in which district he may live.

Roughly, cloche-covered crops have from three to five weeks start of those grown wholly without protection and at the other end of the season they may prolong crops from two to four weeks. Even if they are used only for covering the seeds or seedlings temporarily it will increase their earliness considerably and in cold districts it may also mean the difference between growing a crop and not growing it at all. For instance, in the colder northern counties such crops as French beans and tomatoes may have to be planted so late that just as they are getting into their stride they are cut down by frost. In industrial districts, too, with heavy atmospheric pollution and in districts of high rainfall the cloches act like umbrellas and keep dirt and searing acid off the foliage and out of the hearts of the plants.

Beginners may be put off cloches by their apparent fragility but it is amazing how much they will stand up to if placed evenly and correctly on the soil.

Cloches should be kept clean and stored on their ends during high summer when not in use and when placed over a crop, care should be taken to see that they do not ride on the glass of the adjoining cloches. When placing them over crops it pays to draw a shallow V-shaped drill on each side of the crop to be covered, the exact width of the crop, and set the edges of the cloche in this. Fill in the outer side of the drill again and it will be found that after the first shower of rain the cloches will be firmly held by suction and will withstand gales of up to 80 miles an hour.

As a general rule there are fewer weeds and less disease under cloches as the surface of the soil underneath is always dry, all watering is done from the outside and this seeps under the roots. For seed sowing, the cloche may be regarded as a miniature greenhouse and if the seed is sown directly into the ground then the cloches should be placed over the site of the drill about 10–14 days beforehand to allow it to warm up. Cloches may also be used either to cover seedlings raised in boxes in the greenhouse or used to cover seed sown in boxes and placed under them to germinate. Even in northern counties a start can be made with the sowing of lettuces and carrots under cloches in Feburary when the soil outside may be frozen hard.

120   Crop variations and systems of cropping to utilise the cloche to

its best advantage are many but the most common method for the ordinary gardener is to cover say a row of peas until they are nicely up and then move them over an adjoining crop which is newly sown. Always move if possible to the windward side so that the crop from which they have been removed may enjoy the sideways protection even when over another crop.

For tender plants such as marrows, melons, cucumbers and tomatoes to which a touch of frost is death, they are invaluable and for this purpose they should be regarded as individual covers and fitted with end glasses. No book will teach cloche gardening so it is suggested that a few be acquired with which to gain experience in use and handling and then to extend the range. Purchasing a large batch after reading some enthusiastic literature is, in my opinion the surest way to failure. Cloches are excellent servants and their timely use will most certainly be valuable but can be an expensive luxury if not used wisely.

Vegetable Garden

7   Facts and Figures

How much seed is needed.

Quantities given are approximate, but sown thinly and evenly generally in separate stations, to economise with seed at the rates given, not much thinning out should be necessary.

Subject	*Seeds for 50ft. of row*
Beans, Broad.	$\frac{1}{2}$ pint.
Beans, Dwarf French.	$\frac{1}{4}$ pint.
Beans, Haricot.	$\frac{1}{4}$ pint.
Beans, Runner.	$\frac{1}{2}$ pint.
Beet Sea kale.	$\frac{1}{4}$ ounce.
Beetroot, Globe.	$\frac{1}{4}$ ounce.
Carrot.	$\frac{1}{4}$ ounce.
Lettuce.	$\frac{1}{8}$ ounce.
Onions.	$\frac{1}{4}$ ounce.
Parsnip.	$\frac{1}{4}$ ounce.
Peas.	$\frac{1}{4}$ pint.
Radish.	$\frac{1}{2}$ ounce.
Spinach, Summer.	$\frac{1}{4}$ ounce.
Spinach, Winter.	$\frac{1}{4}$ ounce.
Swede.	$\frac{1}{4}$ ounce.
Turnip.	$\frac{1}{4}$ ounce.

Seeds sown in seed bed, seedlings to be transplanted.

Subject	*Seeds to supply* 100 *plants*
Borecole.	$\frac{1}{8}$ ounce.
Broccoli.	$\frac{1}{8}$ ounce.
Brussels Sprouts.	$\frac{1}{8}$ ounce.
Cabbage.	$\frac{1}{8}$ ounce.
Cauliflower.	$\frac{1}{8}$ ounce.
Celery.	$^1/_{32}$ ounce.
Cucumbers.	100.
Leek.	$\frac{1}{16}$ ounce.
Onion for transplanting.	$\frac{1}{16}$ ounce.
Savoys.	$\frac{1}{16}$ ounce.
Tomatoes.	$\frac{1}{8}$ ounce.
Vegetable Marrow.	100.

Germination time for vegetables.

Subject	Time
Beans, Broad.	10–12 days.
Beans, Runner.	10–12 days.
Beet.	15–24 days.
Brussels Sprouts.	8–15 days.
Cabbage.	8–15 days.
Carrots.	15–24 days.
Cauliflowers.	8–12 days.
Leeks.	18–24 days.
Lettuce.	10–15 days.
Onion, Spring Sown.	18–24 days.
Onion, Autumn Sown.	12–21 days.
Parsnip.	18–28 days.
Peas.	18–24 days.
Radish.	6–12 days.
Spinach.	10–16 days.
Tomato.	8–15 days.
Turnip.	8–12 days.
Vegetable Marrow.	5–12 days.

The Exhibiting and Judging of Vegetables.

The Royal Horticultural Society publishes The Horticultural Show Handbook, which is a first class publication for exhibitors, judges and schedule-makers. Many vegetables are judged on their points value and the following details are therefore given as a help to both old and new vegetable exhibitors. The information is given by permission of the Royal Horticultural Society.

In assessing the merits of exhibits of vegetables the following features should usually be considered: condition, size and uniformity.

Condition, i.e. cleanliness, freshness, tenderness and presence or absence of coarseness and blemishes.

Size is meritorious if accompanied by quality (but only in those circumstances) as the production of large specimens of good quality requires more skill than the production of small specimens. The size of vegetables most suitable for table use varies with the consumer.

Uniformity, i.e. the state of being alike in size, form and colour.

Maximum points for a dish. The exhibition value of any kind of vegetable is governed by the difficulty of producing a perfect dish. The maximum points for a perfect dish will be as follows:

Maximum points awarded in Collections of Vegetables.

Artichokes, Globe	20	Leeks	20
Beans, Broad	15	Lettuces	15
Beans, Dwarf French	18	Marrows	10
Beans, Scarlet Runner	18	Onions	20
Beet	15	Parsnips	15
Brussels Sprouts	15	Potatoes	20
Cabbage	15	Radishes	10
Carrots	20	Shallots	10
Cauliflowers	20	Sweet Corn	10
Celery	20	Tomatoes	20
Cucumbers	18	Turnips	15

Where exhibiting a Collection of vegetables it is obviously advisable where possible to enter those vegetables which have the highest points value.

Rhubarb—forced